# MAKE YOUR OWN
# TOOLBOX

## A Woodworker's Guide to Building Chests, Cases & Cabinets

From the Editors of **Popular Woodworking**

CEDAR LANE PRESS

# CONTENTS

Page 6

## 1. PORTABLE

Tool Tote                                    6

Stacking Tool Caddy                          9

Hardware Hideaway                           16

A Traveler's Tool Case                      23

Authentic Sloyd Tool Cabinet                27

Traveling Tool Chest                        42

One for the Road                            51

Traveling Toolbox                           58

## 2. CHESTS

Machinist's Tool Chest                      66

Dovetailed, Curly Maple Tool Chest          74

10-Drawer Tool Chest                        84

12 Rules for Tool Chests                    91

Tommy Mac's Toolbox                        100

Dutch Tool Chest                           108

## 3. RACKS & CABINETS

Portable Chisel Rack                       120

Tool Rack                                  125

Saw & Plane Till                           129

Roy Underhill's Nail Cabinet               137

Handplane Cabinet                          146

Cabinet Maker's Tool Chest                 157

Not-So-Ordinary Router Cabinet             168

Arts & Crafts Tool Cabinet                 178


Contributors                               190

Manufacturers                              190

Index                                      191

Page 91

# PORTABLE

**Toolboxes that travel with you.** Sometimes, a project requires on-site work, far away (or far enough away) from your usual workshop and bench space. The smaller size of the projects in this section lend themselves to convenient and managable voyaging. These boxes satisfy the need to safely transport the necessities without your tools clanging together, causing dulled edges and dinged handles. Whether the task at hand is simply in a different room of your house, at a friend or family member's place, or a plane ride away, there is a portable option here for you.

# TOOL TOTE

## Wedged through-tenons keep this handle secure.

BY MEGAN FITZPATRICK

Whether you're using it for woodworking tools or garden tools, a tote is a simple and quick project. It's so simple, in fact, that I decided to add a wee degree of difficulty with a curved handle secured in place by wedged through-tenons. And, I wrapped the handle with suede for a more comfortable and secure grip.

### A QUICK TRIP TO THE LUMBER AISLE

This tote is made from dimensional S4S lumber, available at any home center. I chose pine because a) it's inexpensive, b) the poplar looked like beavers had gnawed it to size, and c) red oak is too heavy—especially after you load the tote with tools.

You need to buy only two pieces of wood: a 6'-long 1x8 and a 2'-long 1x4. While it's always best to pick through the rack for the straightest, best-looking lumber you can find, in the case of this 1x4, it's particularly important because it will be hard to fit the through-tenons if the handle stock isn't straight.

### AN EXERCISE IN CHAMFERING

First, set up a stop block at the miter saw to cut the two side pieces to 22" in length. Then move the stop block and cut the two 13"-tall ends. Cut the handle stock to 22 ¼" in length.

Now, pick the show face of your sides and use your block plane to chamfer each edge—first knock off the four corners to avoid spelching.

This is a tool tote—not a piece of furniture—so it's a good opportunity to practice "freehand" chamfering. Hold your block plane at a consistent angle and keep making passes until you like the way the chamfer looks. If you simply must have perfect chamfers (and don't trust your freehand skills), mark a line ⅛" back from the corner around the edges, and again around the face, then plane down to your layout lines on both.

Next, lay out the through-mortises and curves on your two end pieces. First, strike a centerline. The ¾" x 1½" mortise is centered side to side, and starts 1¼" down from the top edge. Mark it on both sides of the workpiece.

The top point of the curve on my sides starts at a point 1" to either side of the centerline, and terminates flush where the side pieces will join the end pieces (so that's 7¼" from the bottom). Join the two points with a curve that looks good to your eye (I used a 5-gallon bucket as a template).

With the layout complete, cut the curves with a jigsaw and use a rasp to refine the shape as needed before sanding smooth.

## THROUGH-MORTISES

Clamp the workpiece flat on your workbench and lightly define the edges of your mortise with a chisel, then lift out the shallow chip of waste (the beveled side of the chisel should always face the waste area). Now chop halfway through the workpiece, remove the waste, then flip and repeat until your mortise meets in the middle. Do the same on end two.

When working with ¾" pine and on such a small mortise, I see no ben-

**Chop chop.** First, use light taps to define the edges of your mortise, then lift out a thin wafer of waste (left). Chop around the mortise, working halfway through your workpiece; remove the waste (below). Flip the workpiece over and repeat.

**Scrap trammel.** It's simple to make a trammel to lay out large curves, such as the handle. Drill a pencil hole at one end of a flat, straight piece of scrap. Measure the distance of the diameter of the required circle (in this case, 16"), and use a nail to secure the other end of the stick to a piece of scrap the same thickness as your workpiece. Line up the trammel on the centerline of your workpiece, then mark the curve.

**Wedgie.** After using a handsaw to cut a kerf in the center of each end of the handle, paint your wedges with glue and tap them in. After the glue dries, trim the wedge flush with the end of the handle.

## EXPLODED VIEW

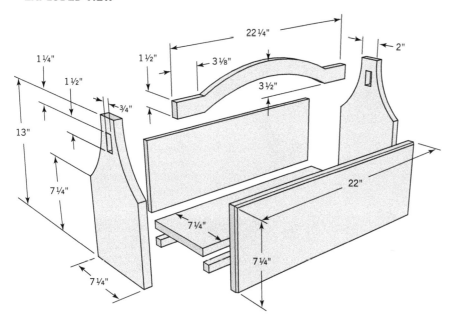

The curved portion is an arc of a 16"-diameter circle—too big for my compass. So, I made a down and dirty trammel to mark the curve (see the photo on p. 7).

You know what comes next: Cut out the handle using your jigsaw, then use a rasp and sandpaper to refine the shape. (Clamp a straightedge to the work to use as a sawguide for the straight cuts.)

Dry fit the ends through the mortises, using your block plane or sandpaper to adjust the tenons as needed. They should go in with light hand pressure. With the tenons fit, remove the handle and saw a 5/16"-deep kerf across each end. Cut wedges from a scrap of 3/4"-thick hardwood using your handsaw.

### ASSEMBLE

Glue and nail a cleat at the bottom interior edge of each side piece. Make sure the handle ends are inserted through the mortises, line up the sides and ends so everything is flush, and clamp the box together. Drill three pilot holes at each corner; nail the box together with 6d finish nails.

Paint glue on the thin end of the wedges, insert them in the kerfs at either handle end then alternate ends as you tap the wedges until they're fully seated (this will help keep the handle centered in the box). After the glue dries, cut the wedge flush with the tenon.

Cut the bottom to fit, and slip it in place (take a few passes with your block plane along one long edge as needed).

Sand to #120 grit and paint, then wrap the handle with some suede. Now your tools can travel in style. ■

## CUT LIST & MATERIALS

| | NO. | ITEM | DIMENSIONS (INCHES) | | | MATERIAL |
|---|---|---|---|---|---|---|
| | | | T | W | L | |
| ☐ | 2 | Sides | 3/4 | 7 1/4 | 22 | 1x8 pine |
| ☐ | 2 | Ends | 3/4 | 7 1/4 | 13 | 1x8 pine |
| ☐ | 1 | Bottom | 3/4 | 7 1/4 | 20 1/2 | 1x8 pine |
| ☐ | 1 | Handle | 3/4 | 3 1/2 | 22 1/4 | 1x4 pine |
| ☐ | 2 | Cleats | 3/4 | 3/4 | 20 | Scrap |
| ☐ | 1 | Handle wrap | | | | Suede |

efit to drilling out the majority of the waste. Pine is easy to chop—I can be done in the time it takes me to find the proper-size bit and drill a series of holes.

### GET A HANDLE ON IT

My handle is 1 1/2" in width along the entire length and the straight area at both ends is 3 1/8" long. But before you lay out your handle, measure your mortises and adjust the handle width to fit.

# STACKING TOOL CADDY

**This simple-to-build tote is perfect for tool and supplies transport.**

BY CHAD STANTON

I designed this stacking tool caddy to hold small parts and a few tools. It comprises three tool trays that stack and interlock together to form a single unit that can be carried wherever needed. Best of all, it stores my screws, nails, and small tools so they're all right at hand. It's also handy for transporting other items: sewing supplies, fishing tackle, and whatever else you can think up.

The trays are joined with half-laps secured by dowels. The dowels add strength and a decorative detail

**Matching lengths.** For clean cuts and a good registration surface, attach an auxiliary fence to the stock fence of the miter saw. Also, ensure consistent lengths by using a stop block. With the saw off, measure from the blade to the block, and clamp it in place. Start by cutting the end of the board square, then put that end against the stop and make your cuts.

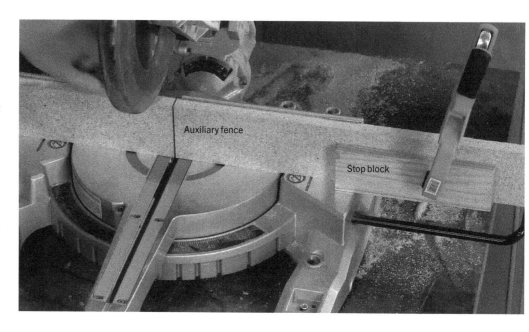

Auxiliary fence

Stop block

## CUT LIST & MATERIALS

| | NO. | ITEM | DIMENSIONS (INCHES) | | | MATERIAL |
|---|---|---|---|---|---|---|
| | | | T | W | L | |
| ☐ | 6 | Tray sides | ½ | 3½ | 19½ | ½x4 poplar |
| ☐ | 6 | Tray ends | ½ | 3½ | 8½ | ½x4 poplar |
| ☐ | 3 | Tray bottoms | ½ | 8½ | 19 | Plywood |
| ☐ | 2 | Handle arms | ¾ | 1½ | 14¾ | Walnut |
| ☐ | 1 | Handle | ¾-dia. | | 21½ | Walnut dowel |
| ☐ | 1 | Top tray divider | ¾ | 5½ | 18½ | Walnut |
| ☐ | 1 | Middle tray divider | ¾ | 3 | 18½ | Walnut |
| ☐ | 2 | Handle stops | ⅜-dia. | | 1 | Dowel |
| ☐ | 2 | Handle spring latches | ⅛ | ⅝ | 4* | Tongue depressor |
| ☐ | 1 | Joinery dowel | ¼-dia. | | † | Walnut |
| ☐ | 2 | Bolts | ¼-20 | | 1½ | |
| ☐ | 6 | Washers | ¼-20 | | | |
| ☐ | 2 | Nuts | ¼-20 | | | |

* Cut to fit. † Length varies—48" should be enough, but buy more to account for error.

to the project. To lock the trays together, the main handle pivots, allowing access to the individual trays.

### TRAYS FIRST
The sides for each tray are ½" x 3½" poplar (dimensional ½x4 lumber from the big box store). To begin the construction, cut the side and end pieces. It's vital they are the same length—if they aren't, the trays won't be square and won't stack and interlock correctly. A stop block can aid in making the repeat cuts accurately. Cut the short tray ends, then reset the stop block to cut the long tray sides—you should have six of each.

Next, rout a ¼" x ¼" rabbet on each end of each of the tray pieces for the half-lap joinery. Watch out—the router bit has a tendency to fracture and tear out the fibers as you exit the cut, leaving a jagged corner. An easy way to eliminate the blowout is to first make a small cut with a handsaw to define the exit point of the bit.

Next, glue up the trays. It can be tricky to hold the tray together and glue each side at the same time. To make it less of a juggling act, use some painter's tape to temporarily hold the joint together while you apply glue to the other corners.

Before the glue dries, place the tray in clamps snugly, but not fully tightened, so you can check for square. Measure diagonally from corner to corner one way, then the other—the measurements should be the same. If they're off, that means the tray is slightly racked and has to be adjusted. Once you've got it where you want it, slowly and evenly tighten the clamps. Check for square one more time before allowing the glue to set up.

With the glue dry, make sure the top and bottom edges are all flat and flush. If necessary, use a block plane to true them up. Cut a ¼" rabbet on the top and bottom edges—you can use the same router setup as you did for the joinery.

The corners of the rabbets will be round. Use a chisel to square these so that the bottoms' corners will seat fully and so the trays nest together in a stack.

Next, cut the ½" plywood bottoms to length and width. Because the rabbets are only ¼" deep, the plywood sits below the sides by ¼"—this lets the bottom register into the top of the tray below. However, the lowest tray's bottom should not project—it should be flush with the side pieces. Use the router with the same bit and depth setting to cut a ¼" rabbet on all four edges of the bottom for the bottom tray. The rabbets on the tray bottom and tray sides will nest

**Rabbet.** Rout the rabbets on the ends of every tray part. I use a bench hook to hold the work in place and off the bench.

**Router setup.** Use a ¼" rabbet bit for the joinery. The bit will automatically make a ¼" cut in width because of the bearing size, but the bit still has to be set so it's cutting ¼" down from the base plate.

together, allowing the bottom to sit flush with the sides. Make sure when routing the outside of the workpiece that you're moving clockwise around the work. Now glue in the plywood bottoms.

Next, reinforce the joinery with some ¼" dowels by drilling three holes in from the sides through each joint. Refer to the drawings for layout—they are ¼" from the ends, and should be evenly spaced. The end grain will want to blow out during this operation—there are a few ways to prevent that from happening.

**TOP VIEW**

**SIDE VIEW**

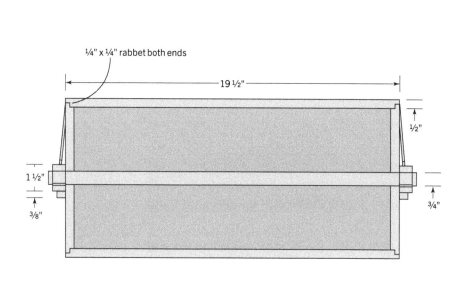

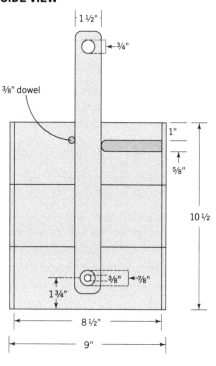

¼" x ¼" rabbet both ends

19 ½"

½"

1 ½"

⅜"

¾"

1 ½"

¾"

⅜" dowel

1"

⅝"

10 ½

3⁄8"  ←7⁄8"

1 ¾"

8 ½"

9"

**FRONT VIEW**

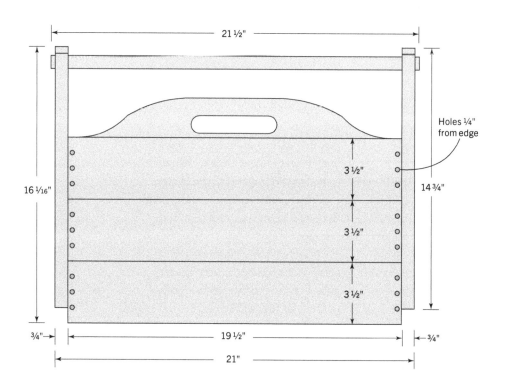

21 ½"

Holes ¼"
from edge

3 ½"

3 ½"

3 ½"

14 ¾"

16 1⁄16"

¾"

19 ½"

¾"

21"

First, place some tape over the corner to reinforce the fibers while drilling. Also, carefully measure and draw the lines where the dowels should be placed to avoid getting too close to the sides of the boards. Lastly, make sure the drill is up to full speed before pushing down into the wood, or it will tend to tear at the fibers instead of cutting them cleanly.

After drilling all the holes, glue in the dowels. To make sure you have the right length of dowel for each hole, keep the dowel long and glue it in one hole at a time. Put glue in the hole and on the end of the dowel rod, then tap the dowel until it's seated. With a flush-cut saw, flush the dowel to the tray surface. Repeat the process for all the tray sides.

### GET A HANDLE ON IT
The top divider has a tall handle, and the middle divider has a low handle that sits below its walls. From the drawing on page 15, make full-sized templates for the two dividers and trace them onto the wood. Use a jigsaw or other appropriate saw (such as a bowsaw or bandsaw) to rough out the shape.

Start the finger holds by drilling the outermost holes, then drill several holes in a line between them. Place a sacrificial piece of wood underneath to prevent drilling into your benchtop. Also, clamp the workpiece to the scrap when drilling—this will prevent blowout on the other side of the workpiece as the drill bit exits the wood.

Chisel to your layout lines, removing the waste left from drilling. Chop about halfway into the work, then flip the board over and finish the

**Rout again.** Cut a ¼" x ¼" rabbet on the inside of the top and bottom of the trays, after the glue dries. The router bit and setting are the same as for the joints. When routing on the inside of a piece, make sure to move the router clockwise—you should always move the router so the rotation of its bit is against the direction you're moving.

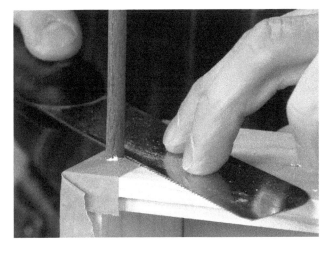

**Add dowels.** Keeping the dowel long assures you'll bottom out on each hole. After applying glue and tapping it home, cut off the excess with a flush-cut saw.

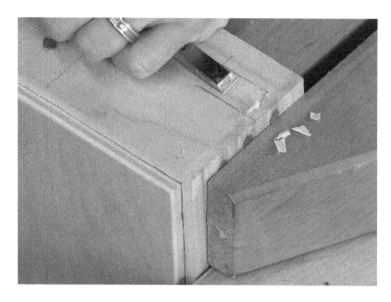

**Install spring latches.** The mortises that hold the spring latches are pared with a chisel held at an angle to form a ramp (top). This causes them to stand proud (bottom). A tongue depressor is just the right size and thickness, but any thin piece of wood will work.

work. This will give you better results because by working from both sides, the back side won't blow out. File and sand to make the divider's curves and finger holds smooth and comfortable to the touch.

To mount the dividers in the tray, find the centers of the tray sides and, with the divider clamped in place, drill ¼" holes from the outside of the tray into the divider. Use ¼" dowel and glue to secure the divider. Both dividers are affixed in the same way.

Before you make the larger exterior handle, make the spring latches and handle stops. The spring latches are made from tongue depressors, which flex to secure the handle vertically. The stops are pieces of dowel that prevent the handle from rotating too far.

From the plans, lay out the lines for the spring latches on the top tray's sides and use a knife to score deep lines to define each latch's mortise.

With a chisel, pare away the wood between the knife cuts at a gradual slope so the mortise angles upward. Test each latch as you chisel its slot—it should be proud enough to hold the handle back but easy to press down far enough to allow the handle to pass over. Use glue and small brads to secure the spring latches in place.

The handle stops are ⅜" dowels drilled and glued in place. They should be installed so that the handle stops vertically, after passing over the latches.

Now, while the glue for the spring latches and stops is drying, make the main handle. This handle is mounted to the lowest tray by a nut and bolt through the arm and into the tray. The two arms of the handles on either side are connected by a ¾" dowel above the stacking trays.

Cut the arms to length and drill a ⅞" hole part of the way through the bottom of each arm. This will allow the bolt heads to sit below the surface. On the same centers, drill through the arms with a ⅜" bit, and drill a corresponding ⅜" hole into the sides on the lowest tray.

Then drill a ¾" hole all the way through the top of each arm, through which the ¾" dowel will pass to connect the two arms together. Round over and smooth the corners of the arms with a file or sandpaper.

Place a 1½"-long x ¼"-20 bolt and washer through the handle arm on each side. Sandwich another washer between the arms and the sides of the tray, then a washer and nut on the inside of the tray. The nuts might have a tendency to come loose during use, so use cyanoacrylate (such as Loctite) on the bolts before threading the nuts on.

With the bolts tightened and in place, assemble the stacking trays and move the main handle into place. Glue in the ¾" dowel for the main handle. Leave it a little long for now.

With the dowel in place, but before the glue dries, make the final adjustments on the handle. The arms should be locked in place by the spring latches but still able to pass over them when they're depressed. Adjust the clearance by moving the arms closer or spreading them apart from one another. Once the clearance is correct, let the glue dry, then cut the ends of the dowel flush to the arms. A nail can be driven through the arm into the dowel to further reinforce the joint between the two.

**TRAY DIVIDERS & HANDLE ARMS**
One square = 1"

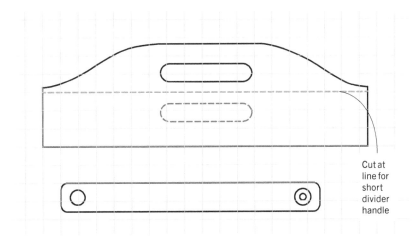

Cut at line for short divider handle

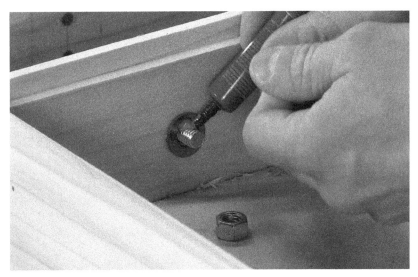

**Add hardware.** Attach the handle with the 1 ½"-long x ¼"-20 bolts. I'm using Loctite to keep the nuts from loosening—once dry, it acts as a mild glue, but can be reversed with some persuasion.

Lastly, sand and finish the parts. I used a simple oil/varnish blend—it applies easily with a rag and gives a soft lustre and a protective finish that isn't too thick. The thin film prevents the finish from chipping or sticking when the trays are stacked together. ◼

# HARDWARE HIDEAWAY

**Store handles, hinges, and fasteners
in this handsome dust-free organizer.**

BY GLEN D. HUEY

**W**hile exploring in an antique store, I found a small, two-level lidded box that would be ideal to store the loads of extra hardware I have stowed in plastic bags. No longer would I need to search endlessly for brads, bails, and back plates; everything would be in one place.

The price of the antique, however, was too rich for my wallet, so I took a photo and used the "dollar bill" method of measuring (i.e., a piece of United States paper money is approximately 6" in length). Even if my memory was defective, my notes, measurements and pirated photo could get me close.

## BUILD THE JIG

Both the box and the tray, which fits inside and rests on the lower layer of cubbies, are assembled using box joints (also called finger joints) that I cut at the table saw. Box joints have plenty of glue surface for a strong bond, but are easier than dovetails to whip out by machine. In fact, they are perfect for shop builds. (The same basic process is also a great technique for making dentil molding.)

Mill the sides and ends of both the box and tray to size and thickness, then set them aside and set up your table saw for making box joints.

First, attach a sacrificial fence to your miter gauge. Install a dado stack set at ½" wide, and raise the depth of cut to ½". Make a single pass of the gauge and fence over the stack to establish the notch for the jig's key—the piece that guides the box joint–making process.

Mill a 12"-long stick of scrap that exactly fits the width and height of the notch (mine is ½" square; I milled it at the planer), then cut a 3"-long piece (the key) to fit and attach into the fence's notch. A couple of brads hold the key in place. With the remaining stick held tight to the right side of the table saw blade (see bottom right), free the sacrificial fence from the miter gauge, slide the installed key so it's tight to the right-hand side of the stick, then re-attach the fence to the miter gauge. The jig is ready to go. (As always, you should make a test cut to confirm that your joints will be tight…or not.)

For the sides of the box, begin with the workpiece positioned tight to the left-hand side of the key. Run the assembly over the dado stack to make the first notch in your workpiece, spaced ½" from the edge of the board. Slip the newly cut notch over the key and make another pass. Repeat these steps until you've reached the opposite edge of the board, then flip the board to cut the opposite end. Cut the fingers on the second side, too.

To cut joinery on the ends, begin with the edge of your workpiece set even with the right-hand edge of the fence cutout; with the first cut, you remove the corner of the board. That corner notch then slips over the key and the balance of the end piece is cut in repetitive passes.

Tray parts are cut the same way, but before any work is done, tweak the blade height to 9/16". Your first pass raises the cut area, but doesn't affect anything else in the setup. The idea is to slightly reduce the size of the tray to make it easier to lift the unit in and out of the box. Just as before, begin with the tray sides then finish up with the ends.

Dry-assemble the box and tray. Your fit should be tight, but not too tight. If you're working with pine as I am, there is a bit of a "smash factor" you can count on. Be more particular when using hardwoods.

### DADOS ADD STRENGTH

Each side of both the box and the tray has two dados for the ¼"-thick bin dividers; the dados are almost equally spaced along the lengths (see the illustration on p. 21 for more information). The ends have a single dado that's cut dead center. I use a shop-made jig to guide my router and ¼" spiral-upcut router bit to cut the dados (see "Simple & Accurate Router Jig" on p. 19).

The layout work is easy. For the sides, measure the length between the joint work, then divide the result by three. Make a mark at the two locations. For the ends, find the centerline of the piece (measure between the joinery) and place a mark. Move ⅛" in both directions off

**Simple setup.** Setup for box joints is easy: A sacrificial fence and a milled stick work like magic, as long as you dial in your settings.

**Make the first cuts.** The finger cuts for the box and tray sides begin with the workpiece tight to the left-hand side of the key.

**Make the mates.** I use the milled stick as a spacer for this step; it takes out any guess-work.

**Cut dados.** Router-cut dados help to align the bin dividers and increase the overall strength of the box and tray.

**Watch your fingers.** It's a good idea to clamp your box and tray, but as you do, make sure the fingers, which are slightly proud of the face of the units, are not captured underneath.

to all the fingers then slip the sides and ends together. A couple of light mallet taps should set the joints tight—but it doesn't hurt to add a few clamps. Make sure they don't catch the fingers, which are slightly proud of the face of the units.

When the glue is dry, plane or sand the fingers flush to the sides and ends.

### DIVIDE AND CONQUER

Mill the dividers to size and thickness, leaving the parts a bit longer than needed. Using the assembled box and tray to measure, square one end of a divider, set the end into a dado, then mark and cut the opposite end. (A well-tuned miter saw is perfect for this.) Cut the four pieces for the short dividers, and the two pieces for the longer dividers.

Use an egg-crate joint to assemble the interior of the two units. To mark the location of the cuts, I find it better to use the box or tray itself. Set the part—short dividers at the ends and longer dividers at the sides—in position on the box or tray. Make sure you align the dividers with the back of the dado slot. When positioned, mark both edges of the dado onto the dividers.

The slots for the egg-crate joints are best cut with another table saw jig. This setup is simply a sacrificial fence with a ¼"-thick carrier attached to its bottom edge. Attach the unit to your miter gauge so the blade cuts the jig about 2" from the end. Raise the blade to just reach the center of the divider—don't forget to account for the carrier thickness. Once set, make a pass over the blade to cut the ⅛"-wide slot. That slot is key when using the jig.

the marks to lay in the location of the bin dividers.

The dados in the box parts extend up from the bottom edge 2"; those in the tray are routed completely through the parts. Use a backer board to keep from blowing out the grain as the router bit exits the cuts.

After you've cut the dados, use a ¼"-wide chisel to square the ends of the box dados, then assemble the box and tray. To take full advantage of the box joint's strength, apply glue

## SIMPLE & ACCURATE ROUTER JIG

One of the most useful shop-made router jigs I use is for cutting small dados. (This setup is best used on workpieces no wider than 10".) Make a jig for each router and router bit pairing; different combinations require different jigs. My shop is awash with them.

Each jig requires three parts: base, guide fence, and T-square. Each part comes from small pieces or scraps. For the base, I like ¼" plywood, but I've used Masonite and even pegboard in a pinch. The fence is usually a piece of ¾"-thick hardwood that's 1" wide, and my T-square material is most often ½" thick, but sometimes I use ¾".

To begin, load a spiral-upcut bit into your router, then measure the distance from the edge of the router base to the center of the bit; approximate measurements are great, but err to the heavy side. Add 1" to your size. Grab a piece of plywood that's the width needed and a couple of inches longer than your workpiece to use as the base, then attach a guide fence to one edge—I use small brads and glue.

Hold the assembly with the fence to the left-hand side and run the router with its base tight to the fence. Your bit cuts the base and establishes the exact place of the cut each time the jig is used.

Using a square, align the T-square piece at 90° to the just-cut edge, so that its end sits flush or just behind the edge of the base. When set, attach the ½"-thick part to the assembly using brads. Be careful—you're driving fasteners through a thin material.

To use the jig, align its right-hand edge even with your layout line, and keep the T-square tight to the workpiece. Clamp the jig and workpiece secure, then set the bit's depth of cut—remember that you need to reach beyond the thickness of the jig's base—and rout the dado. It's easy to align, accurate, and works every time.

**Dial-in the location.** Running the router up the assembled jig cuts the jig exactly where the edge of the router bit does its work.

**Get it square.** The usefulness of this jig depends on the T-square piece being set at a perfect 90° to the base.

**In action.** Here you see the dado jig in action—you also see a backer that eliminates any blow-out as you cut the tray parts.

Position your divider on the carrier and against the fence, align the right-most mark at the right edge of the slot—you can easily see the slot cut in the carrier—then make a pass. To complete the egg-crate cut, slide the left-most layout mark to the left side of the carrier slot and make the cut. If your layout marks

are accurate, the newly formed slot should slip over the thickness of any divider. If it doesn't, no worries. Set the divider back on the jig and tweak your slot opening—the edge of the carrier slot easily identifies where to position your divider.

Make the egg-crate slot in each divider. It matters not whether you

cut the slots in the top edge, the bottom edge or both. The bin dividers are generic as they fit to the box and tray.

After you've cut and fit your dividers, assemble the pieces in the box and tray. Glue adds little but a mess, so I forego its use here. The box dividers slip in from the bottom; tray parts fit in any direction. As you fit the

**Two procedures.** Set the parts—short dividers at the ends and longer dividers at the sides—in position on the box or tray as you transfer the layout.

**In plain view.** Drawing a bead on where to position your egg-crate cuts is straightforward because you can easily see the slot cut in the carrier.

**Easy does it.** Your egg-crate joints should slip together easily with finger pressure only (and glue is overkill).

center pieces in place, you may need to gently bend or twist the shorter dividers to get the egg-crates joined. If you need stronger measures, check the layout and cuts for problems.

The bottoms of the box and tray are ¼"-thick plywood. Cut the bottoms to fit, add a thin bead of glue around the perimeter, position the plywood, then nail the bottom in place. Don't attempt to nail the dividers. I use an 18-gauge brad, but

a 23-gauge pin works just fine. (Keep the fastener length to a minimum; you don't want to risk bending a brad or pin so it pierces the outside face of your box or tray.)

### NO NASTY CORNERS

Each cubby has a small piece of chamfered molding wrapping its four sides to make retrieving hardware from the box and tray a snap. The molding is ⅝" x ⅝" and mitered

at the corners. The fit is by friction, although you could add glue as you install each piece.

I make the molding at a router table using a chamfer bit. Begin with a wide workpiece, profile the two edges, then cut the pieces at your table saw, aided by a push stick. As your workpiece gets narrow, it's better to profile from opposing faces so you have a wider support surface riding the saw's table.

**Work small.** As the workpiece narrows, it's better to profile the opposing faces of the stock so you have greater support as you rip at the table saw.

**One setup.** Both ends of the bin moldings can be cut with your miter saw set at 45° to the left—the first cut has the chamfered edge facing front and down.

**Mark alignment.** With your measurement marked on the top edge of the molding, a good set of eyes is all that's needed to dial in the perfect cut.

## 3D VIEW: TRAY

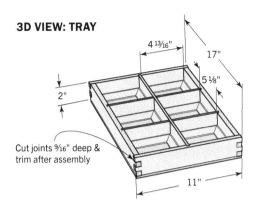

Cut joints ⁹⁄₁₆" deep & trim after assembly

## 3D VIEW

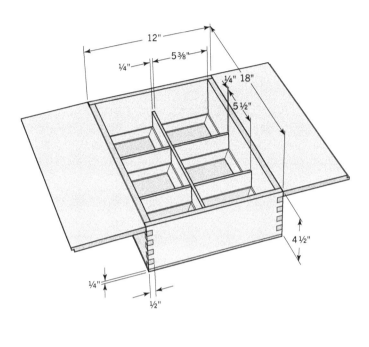

## EXPLODED VIEW: TRAY DIVIDER

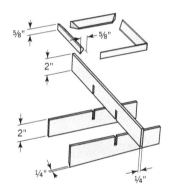

## CUT LIST & MATERIALS

| | NO. | ITEM | DIMENSIONS (INCHES) | | | MATERIAL | COMMENTS |
|---|---|---|---|---|---|---|---|
| | | | T | W | L | | |
| ☐ | 2 | Box sides | ½ | 4½ | 18 | Yellow pine | |
| ☐ | 2 | Box ends | ½ | 4½ | 12 | Yellow pine | |
| ☐ | 1 | Box bottom | ¼ | 12 | 18 | Plywood | |
| ☐ | 1 | Box divider, long | ¼ | 2 | 17⅜ | Yellow pine | |
| ☐ | 2 | Box dividers, short | ¼ | 2 | 11⅜ | Yellow pine | |
| ☐ | 2 | Box lids | ⅝ | 6¼ | 18 | Yellow pine | Shiplap at center. |
| ☐ | 1 | Lid latch | ¼ | ⅞ | 6 | Spalted tamarind | |
| ☐ | 2 | Tray sides | ½ | 2 | 17 | Yellow pine | |
| ☐ | 2 | Tray ends | ½ | 2 | 11 | Yellow pine | |
| ☐ | 1 | Tray bottom | ¼ | 11 | 17 | Plywood | |
| ☐ | 1 | Tray divider, long | ¼ | 2 | 16⅜ | Yellow pine | |
| ☐ | 2 | Tray dividers, short | ¼ | 2 | 10⅜ | Yellow pine | |
| ☐ | 2 | Bin molding | ⅝ | ⅝ | 144 | Yellow pine | |
| ☐ | 2 | Fixed-pin hinges | | | 2 | | |

**Perfect alignment.** The challenge for the top is the shiplap center, but if you cut the joint first, the top is easy to trim to size.

**Fine-tune adjustment.** As the hinges go in, it's possible to slightly reposition the lids—a problem that's easily corrected with a sharp handplane.

**Get square.** I positioned the latch to the box holding it dead center. One screw holds the latch, the other catches it.

Mitering the moldings to fit each cubby could be done by hand, but I favor my chop saw. To make the operation effective, I use double-sided tape to hold a scrap tight at the saw. The scrap holds your cut away from the fence and the saw kerf provides the perfect registration for your cuts.

To work efficiently, you need only to set the saw to 45° to the left. Position one of your chamfered pieces at the chop saw with the ⅝" flats facing up and against the sacrificial fence. Make the first cut.

Measure the length of the piece needed then transfer the length to your molding; to mark an exact layout at its top edge, position the workpiece to your box or tray. Align your mark directly at the kerf in the fence to make the second cut. I found that I occasionally had to trim the pieces to get a press-in fit, but again, the kerf makes it easy to determine where to place your workpiece. Cut and fit the 48 pieces.

## LID AND LATCH

The lid is simply two pieces that are shiplapped at the center. Cut the pieces over-wide, then cut the shiplap (I used a dado stack at the table saw) before you attach the lid to the box with two pair of narrow 2" fixed-pin hinges (available at any hardware store).

Position the two lid pieces on the box and center the joint, then mark and cut the outside edges so the lid fits the box, with a small gap in the middle. (I used two 6" rules as spacers.)

Take your time installing the hardware, and when you've completed the task, use a small plane to even the gap between the lid pieces, if need be. Also, you may need to reduce the width of the hinge leaf attached to the box to facilitate the installation of the tray. I used a file to flush the leaves to the inside of the box.

To hold the box closed, I whipped up a simple wooden latch using a scrap of spalted tamarind, but use whatever you like. Mill the piece to size and length. Drill a slightly oversized hole for a #10 x ⅞" roundhead brass screw in one end of your latch, and cut a slot at the opposite end. Select where you want your latch—I chose the middle of the box—and attach the latch with one of the brass screws. Square the latch to the side of the box, then install the second screw so it fits into the cut-out area of the latch. How much you turn your screws decides how tight the fit. Yes, because they are so noticeable, I clocked these screws.

I decided to allow my box to age naturally, but I used boiled linseed oil on the latch to make sure it stood out. I stripped the zinc coating off the hinges then added a coat of wax.

The box and tray are a great place to store and organize extra pieces of hardware. And this project measures up to my antique-store find, which cost way more than the dollar I used to get sized up on the downlow. ■

# A TRAVELER'S TOOL CASE

## This handy case is the best way for a wayfaring woodworker to bring tools along for the ride.

BY DAVID LYELL AND ANDREW ZOELLNER

When we're moving back and forth between our home shops, the office shop, helping friends, taking classes, and even going on vacation, there are always certain tools we want with us. Each of us has different ideas about what exactly we want and need. Andrew makes do with just a couple chisels; David prefers more sizes. Andrew wants more planes; David just needs a #4 and #5. The point is, this tool case should be customized to exactly how you want to do your work.

The basic design of this tool case has been in use for the last century

**SIDE VIEW**

**3D VIEW**

**FRONT VIEW**

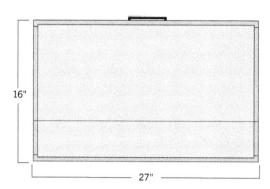

and relies on dovetails for strength. It's referenced by the seminal woodworking writer Charles Hayward a few times, and that's where we first discovered it. The ideal size for this toolbox is about 6" deep, 16" tall, and 27" long, but increasing or decreasing these dimensions by an inch or two is fine. It's big enough to fit a good amount of tools without becoming too unwieldy to be carried by a single person. The length means you could sneak a panel saw into the cabinet (if you need it), and the depth provides space for handplanes, small drawers,

and most other hand tools you rely on to do your work. You can build it out of pine and plywood, or you can use more exotic lumber (you'll just need a few board feet). The sides of the case are about ¾" thick, and the front and back panels are ¼" plywood.

First, though, assemble your tool kit. Typically, when we're out and about woodworking, there's an assumption of things we don't need to bring: most power tools, screwdrivers, sandpaper, and other things that are commonly found in shops. For us, that leaves the tools we use for

| | NO. | ITEM | DIMENSIONS (INCHES) | | | MATERIAL | COMMENTS |
|---|---|---|---|---|---|---|---|
| | | | T | W | L | | |
| ☐ | 2 | Top/bottom | ¾ | 6 | 27 | Maple | |
| ☐ | 2 | Sides | ¾ | 6 | 16 | Maple | |
| ☐ | 1 | Front panel | ¼ | 15 ½ | 26 ½ | Plywood | Leave oversize.* |
| ☐ | 1 | Back panel | ¼ | 15 ½ | 26 ½ | Plywood | Leave oversize.* |
| ☐ | 1 | Dividers | ⅜ | | | Plywood | Cut to fit where desired. |
| ☐ | 1 | Cork | 1⁄16 | ¾ | 55 | Plywood | Cut to fit lid edge. |
| ☐ | 2 | Draw latches | | | | | |
| ☐ | 1 | Handle | | | | | |
| ☐ | 2 | Clips for bottom of lid | | | | Metal | |

**CUT LIST & MATERIALS**

\* It's easiest to cut your plywood to size after you've rabbeted the front and back of the case.

**Lay out and cut your dovetails.** Because we're basically assembling the whole box first and then cutting it apart, you'll want to make sure your cut line goes through a tail, and you'll want that pair of tails to be a bit larger than the rest.

**Rabbet the front and back panels into the sides.** We used the router table and a ¼" bearing-guided rabbeting bit to do this. Rout both sides to final depth (the thickness of your plywood), then square up the corners with a chisel.

**You've built a beautiful box.** Now it's time to cut it apart. We roughed out most of the cuts on the table saw, then finished it off with a hand saw. Make the angled lid cut first, then the two mating cuts, followed by the top edge cut.

**Clean up the cut edges of the lid.** The goal is to have the edges perfectly mate with the lid when closed, to keep out dust and debris and have a nice, even reveal.

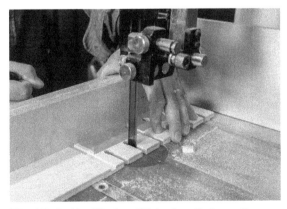

**Fit out the inside of the box.** This is where the fun really begins. This simple chisel holder is just sized so the tang of the chisel fits in the groove.

**BLUE TAPE KEEPS BLOWOUT AT BAY**

We used blue tape on all the plywood edges and on the case to minimize blowout. It's also a handy reference for layout lines and stop lines when it's difficult to see pencil lines.

**Make the interior dividers.** Made from ⅜" plywood, the dividers were cut to fit outside the case, then slid into place. The divider is tacked to the case sides so we can remove and re-adjust later as tool preferences change.

**Install strips of cork.** They replace the material removed from the table saw. Contact cement and a new razor blade will provide a crisp install.

**Here's David's preferred tool kit.** #4 and #5 bench planes, block plane, ¼", ½", ¾" and 1" chisels, marking knife, tape measure, scraper, honing guide, and diamond plate are inside the case. The lid holds a coping saw, dovetail saw, and crosscut saw with the assistance of magnets.

layout, cutting joinery, and refining and finishing projects. Coincidentally, they're also the tools that we're pickiest about.

Once you have your core tools determined, lay out a rectangle on your bench or a sheet of plywood that's 15" tall and 26" long (roughly the interior size of the case), and work through how you'll arrange everything. You'll have about 3" of depth to work with (the typical width of a jointer plane is 3") on the case side. If you need a little bit more or less space, adjust your rectangle. Don't forget about the lid—you'll have an inch or so of depth to hang saws and other tools here, too. Once you've determined your final dimensions, it's time to trim your top, bottom, and ends to size and cut some dovetails.

Now that you have your go-to tools ready to go, get out there and do some woodworking in the wild! ■

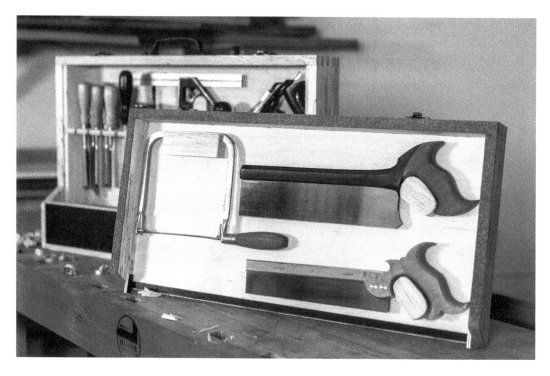

# AUTHENTIC SLOYD TOOL CABINET

## This reproduction is a fun build and a great gift for a budding woodworker.

BY BILL RAINFORD

An early motto of the North Bennet Street Industrial School (NBIS), now called the North Bennet Street School (NBSS), was "Hand and heart lead to life." Founded in 1885 by Pauline Agassiz Shaw, a progressive Boston philanthropist, the school was established to "train students for careers in traditional trades that use hand skills in concert with evolving technology, to preserve and advance craft traditions and promote greater appreciation of craftsmanship."

**Build the box joint jig.** Slide the plywood piece up against two ¼" pin pieces (top). Clamp the plywood to your miter gauge (bottom).

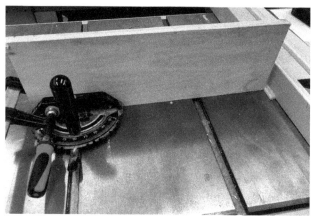

The school started off as a social and educational experiment designed to help residents in the North End of Boston, many of whom were immigrants, acclimate to America, learn a trade, socialize, and become better citizens. In pursuit of this goal, Shaw learned of Otto Salomon's work at the Sloyd School in Naas Sweden and was instrumental in bringing Swedish Educational Sloyd to America. Under the direction of Gustaf Larsson, a graduate of Naas, he helped adapt Educational Sloyd to American needs at NBIS as a training lab and also went on to direct the Sloyd Training School in Boston for training teachers in manual arts instruction. Moving beyond traditional apprenticeships, Educational Sloyd was a structured program wherein hand skills were taught by building a series of model projects, deliberately chosen to result in useful household objects, prescribed in a specific sequence to help bolster hand skills, mental skills, and confidence, and to prepare for the next exercise. The goal was to train the "whole person"—the body and the mind working in concert to produce better work, an appreciation for hand work, and to improve overall well-being.

As a graduate of NBSS, I can say that the core principles of Sloyd are still alive and well at the school even if the term "Sloyd" is not often explicitly used. We started with the fundamentals, taught in a hands-on manner, and built upon those skills until we reached our culminating projects, which involved demonstrating the hand and design skills learned. It served me well as a student and continues to be a part of my own teaching efforts. In the years since I graduated, I've done some research on Sloyd in general and specifically in relation to NBSS and have found it to be a fascinating rabbit hole of discovery.

In teaching students and teachers alike, Larsson designed a novel workbench that went on to be called the "Larsson Improved Sloyd Bench" and was manufactured en masse by Chandler & Barber, which was a large tool supplier in Boston that specialized in manual training supplies that were shipped around the world.

As a companion to that workbench, Chandler & Barber also offered tool sets of varying sizes and combinations, including a handsome set that came in a hand tool cabinet. The cabinet was even advertised in the NBIS alumni newsletter as a "practical holiday gift" for the Sloyder in your life. After learning of the existence of this cabinet when researching Larsson's workbench, I serendipitously stumbled on the only extant example of one of these cabinets I've found to date. We'll walk through how I built my replica of the cabinet and its hardware in this article.

### BUILDING THE CABINET

Start off by milling your cabinet stock. I used clear eastern white pine, but oak would also be appropriate if you want to build the more upscale option. Mill the stock for the cabinet sides, back, top, and bottom to be ½" thick. The fixed shelf in the cabinet and the drawer sides are ⅜" thick. The drawer bottom is ¼" thick. The drawer runners and corner reinforcements are ⁷⁄₁₆" square. From scrap wood, mill a small amount of ¼" square stock we'll use as part of our jig. (You'll want two 2½"-long pieces.)

### FINGER JOINTS

Cut your cabinet sides, top, and bottom to size. Label your parts and explicitly label the inside and outside as it's important when cutting the finger joints to know the orientation. Hold onto any sizeable off-cuts: you can use them to fine tune your finger jointing jig. I used a Freud box joint cutter set, which is similar to a dado set but specifically ground to cut clean shoulders on the box joint fingers. Configure the two blades to cut ¼"-wide fingers and set the height of the blade to ½".

**Cut your first joint.** Keep the board next to the pin.

**Cut the rest.** Use the cut slot to index over the pin and repeat.

**The joinery has been cut for the sides.** Repeat the process for the top and bottom, using a ¼" spacer for the first cut.

Set your rip fence to be 12" to the right of your blade. With some scrap ¾"-thick plywood, cut a 24" x 6" piece we'll use as a sacrificial fence. Place the two ¼"-square, 2½"-long pieces against the rip fence—they should be equal to twice your pin width. Slide the plywood piece up against those two pieces and clamp the plywood to your miter gauge (see p. 28 photos).

Remove the small ¼" pieces. Using this clamped setup and minding your fingers, push the jig through

**Get the right height.** From left to right: blade is too high, blade is too low, blade is the correct height. NOTE: If you have to err on one side, go with longer fingers as you can always sand them off as needed.

## A NEW TOOL CABINET

"The cabinet would be an ornament to any manual training school. The corners of the cabinet are reinforced with steel, and the arrangement of tools convenient. The cabinet contains two saws, steel hammer, Bailey Jack and block and rabbit planes, rule, two chisels, two gouges, screw-driver, bit brace and auger bits, two gimlet bits, screw driver bit,

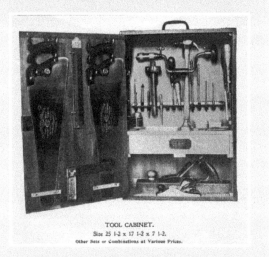

TOOL CABINET.
Size 25 1-2 x 17 1-2 x 7 1-2.
Other Sets or Combinations at Various Prices.

countersink, marking gauge, spoke shave, brad awl, nail set, try square, bevel, half round file, oil stone, oil can, combination pliers, glue, and boxes of assorted brads and screws. It is so constructed that the cover is light, and the cabinet will not fall if resting in a very small space. The heavy lifting handle on top is bolted on the under side so that the cabinet can easily be carried from one place to another. It locks with a level lock and flat key. Chandler and Barber, 15 and 17 Eliot Street, Boston Mass."

the saw. Turn off the saw. Now put one of the ¼" pieces back up against the rip fence, remove the clamp, and carefully slide the fence up against this piece and the fence. Secure the plywood to your miter gauge with screws. Remove the ¼" piece from the fence. Run the jig through the saw again. Turn the saw off. This should produce a nice, evenly spaced set of slots. Glue one of the ¼" pieces in the first slot you made (this is the slot now closer to the fence) and gently chamfer the ends of that alignment pin with some sandpaper. The jig is now complete.

Using the scrap you saved before, let's make some test cuts and fine-tune the jig as needed.

### USING THE JIG

Place your stock on the jig vertically and slide it right until it's firmly against the ¼" piece you glued into the jig. Use a quick clamp to secure the piece as you slide the jig through the blade—keeping your fingers well clear of the blade. Return the jig to your starting position (again, well clear of the blade).

On the next pass you'll move the workpiece to the right by placing the slot in the workpiece over the ¼" alignment pin. Clamp the board and carefully slide the jig through the blade.

Repeat the process of making a slot and moving the board over one notch until you finish cutting all the fingers.

Important note #1: The piece that makes up the other half of this joint will need to start with a pin width offset so the board lines up correctly when assembled. You can do this by putting a ¼" wood spacer between your workpiece and the alignment pin for the first cut on this second board, then clamping the piece to the fence, removing the spacer, and making that first cut. The rest of the procedure is the same as before.

Important note #2: The left side of the cabinet is narrower to accommodate the door; thus, the fingers do not run all the way across the left side top and bottom pieces. Please lay out and plan accordingly.

### FIXED SHELF

Test fit your sides. Once you are happy with the fit it's time to lay out a stopped dado for the fixed shelf in the cabinet. Use a marking knife to sever the cross grain fibers.

Use a chisel and router plane to remove the waste from the stopped dado.

Note: The dado should be about ½" narrower than the width of the shelf (see pp. 31–32). You'll cut a notch into the end of the shelf so that you won't see any exposed dado when the wood moves seasonally.

### CABINET BACK

Now, lay out a dado to capture the back panel of the cabinet. This dado should align with one of the fingers. I used a single box joint cutter blade to accomplish this. Dry fit the sides and shelf and leave that in the clamps (p. 32).

Edge-glue the panels that will form the door and the back of the cabinet. If using flat sawn wood, alter-

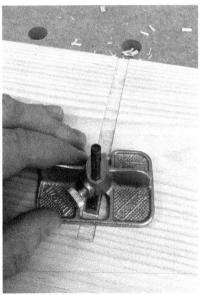

**Lay out the stopped dado (left).** This will capture the fixed shelf. I mark the waste to be cut.

**Removing the waste (right).** The bulk should be removed with a chisel. Flatten the bottom of the dado with a router plane.

**Cut notches.** Because of the stopped dado, the shelf needs notches on both sides of the front edge. I cut these with a handsaw.

**Cut a ¼" dado for the back panel.** Take care to line it up with a finger.

**Prepare the back panel.** The back panel is ½" thick, edge-glued from several boards.

**Cut the rabbet.** Use your table saw to cut the ¼"-deep rabbet around the edges. Fine tune the fit with a shoulder plane.

nate the orientation of the growth rings. Cut the dried panel for the back to size. Cut it slightly narrow to allow for seasonal movement; in sizing the panel, make sure you take into account how it will be captured in the side dadoes.

Using a sacrificial wood fence attached to your rip fence and your stacked dado blade, cut a rabbet into the back panel on all four sides. Tip: Use some scrap from the panel blank to test your setup and make sure it fits nicely into the dado before cutting into your panel.

Test fit your panel on the dry-fit carcase that is still in the clamps. Use a shoulder plane to fine tune the fit and allow room for seasonal expansion of the panel.

Glue and clamp up the carcase, taking care to make sure everything is square and that all the joints pull up nice and tight. I used hot hide glue so any squeeze-out would not affect the finish; hide glue also has a longer open time.

Once dry, plane or sand the fingers flush and round over or radius the corners.

## DOOR

Cut the glued-up door panel to size. Cut the breadboard ends slightly long. Mill a dado down the center of the breadboard end stock using a feather board to help keep things centered (p. 34, bottom photo). Use the same general setup (a dado and sacrificial fence) to mill a tenon onto the top and bottom of the door panel to fit snugly into the breadboard dado. Apply glue to the center third of the breadboard dado and clamp up the door. (This will allow for panel seasonal movement. See p. 33.)

Once dry, flush up the breadboard ends with the rest of the panel and test fit it into the carcase. Use cards or similar spacers to allow for an even spacing around the door top, bottom, and right side and adjust as necessary. (Left side with hinges is flush with the outside of the cabinet.)

## BUILD THE DRAWER

Follow same steps you used to make the carcase to make the drawer and its divider (see p. 35).

Once you have the sides glued up, shoot a pin nail in through the fingers from the bottom to keep the joint together even if the glue fails in the future. (Do the same for the rear of the finger joints on the main cabinet

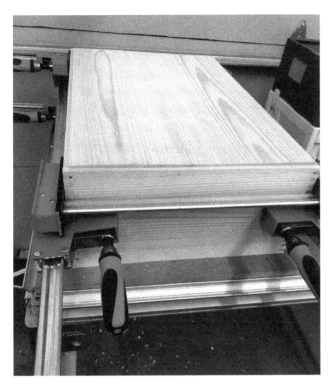

**Dry fit the back and cabinet carcase (top left).** Make sure the pieces are ending up tight and square.

**Size the gap (top right).** The back panel floats in the dado to accommodate seasonal expansion/contraction. Size the rabbet to leave a small (1⁄16") gap on each side.

**Glue up the cabinet (left).** Fit in the panel and shelf. Use hide glue or another glue with a long open time to let you get all the pieces in place and clamped properly.

**Sand the fingers flush.** Add a small roundover on the edges.

**Make a dado.** Mill a dado down the center of the door's breadboard end stock using a feather board to help keep things centered.

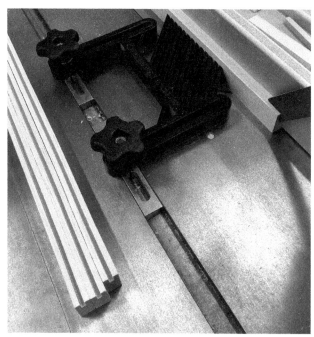

block on the outfeed of your table saw. Place the far end of the drawer up against that stop block and slowly but firmly hinge the drawer down onto the blade. Be very careful when attempting this operation and make sure to do some test cuts first to ensure you are centered and not cutting too deep. Once you make the cut, turn off the saw and wait for it to stop before removing the drawer.

**NOTE ON HARDWARE**

In the late 19th and early 20th century, there was a much wider variety of hardware available in the marketplace. This cabinet has a lot of interesting hardware, much of which you can fashion in your own workshop to provide some interesting tool storage solutions. I also took the time to 'clock' (align) all of the screw heads the same way, which adds a nice touch to this handsome cabinet.

**HANDLE AND LOCK**

Center the brass handle on the top of the cabinet. Transfer the layout of the holes. Pilot-drill through the top and into some scrap wood to prevent blow out. Use 1" brass screws and a washer and doubled up nuts to secure the handle. Trace the lock onto the door; be sure to carefully remove wood and test fit as you go to prevent misalignment. Use a router plane to help excavate the wood. Use a file to remove the mill marks from the brass. Make sure to relieve the wood around the keyhole for a nice, clean look.

**HINGES**

The hinges used on this cabinet are overlay hinges that don't require any mortising (see p. 36). The centerline of

as well.) Glue and pin nail the bottom onto the drawer; test fit and sand as needed. Use two credit cards as spacers between the top of the drawer and the fixed shelf.

Pin nail in a 7/16" square profiled runner on each side to support the drawer. From that same size stock also nail in spacers on the right side of the cabinet to function as a door stop. The drawer divider partitions the space into a 60/40 split.

Once the drawer is complete, you'll want to use a wide stacked dado to cut in a finger grip that functions as a drawer pull. Securely clamp a stop

**Space the drawer under the shelf.** Use cards to space them, then add two square runners under the drawer.

**Cut the hand hold.** I used a wide dado stack in my table saw to cut the hand hold in the bottom of the drawer. Just a shallow recess is enough.

**Cut the mortised lock.** The lock is cut in stages. First, mark the waste (top). Cut the recess for the lock mechanism (center top). Then, cut the shallower portions to get the lock to be inset on the piece (center bottom). Test out the key (bottom).

**Install the hinges.** They are just simple overlay hinges that don't require mortising; just careful layout (top). Test the opening and closing of the lid (bottom).

each hinge is located 4" from the top or bottom of the cabinet, respectively. Be careful not to drill through the cabinet sides or door. Once the hinges are installed, apply some chalk or pencil graphite to the moving portion of the lock bolt, or use some carbon paper and turn the key in the lock to gently press the lock into the side of the cabinet. Using this mark, excavate a small mortise to catch the lock.

## CAST BRASS HOOKS

A pair of cast brass hooks are installed on the back wall of the cabinet to hold your bit brace and another pair are installed on the door to hold your panel saws. Lay out where you want the hardware to be, use a center punch to start the hole, and drill using a depth stop. Install the screws by hand; brass is a soft metal.

## SQUARE HOOKS

Square hooks are used to secure your folding rule and try square to the door. These simple little hooks do a surprisingly good job of keeping those tools in place. When laying out the positions, make sure to use the actual tools for reference; check that they don't interfere with the saws, the drawer, or your ability to close the door.

## FABRIC STRAPS

To keep the panel saws in place, you'll want to cut two 6" pieces of fabric-backed hook-and-loop tape or nylon webbing. Use a lighter to melt the ends. Screw each strap to the cabinet door with some pan head screws and washers for a clean look. When installing the fabric, the center should not be flush with the door;

**Install saw-holding hardware.** I used cast brass hooks to hold my saws, further secured with simple straps. Square hooks hold the ruler and square.

rather, place the screws a little closer together so there is room to easily remove the saw. (I used a hook-and-loop strap I had it on hand from an old backpack; it is stiff and it gives some air to the saw blade, making it less likely to rust.)

## WIRE TOOL HOLDERS

Some of the most interesting hardware pieces in the cabinet are the bent brass wire tool holders. With the help of some fairly simple tools and jigs, you can make custom hardware to hold just about any tool you can imagine (see images on p. 40).

**FRONT VIEW**

**3D VIEW**

**FRONT VIEW (DOOR REMOVED)**

**SIDE VIEW**

**TOOLHOLDER SHAPE**

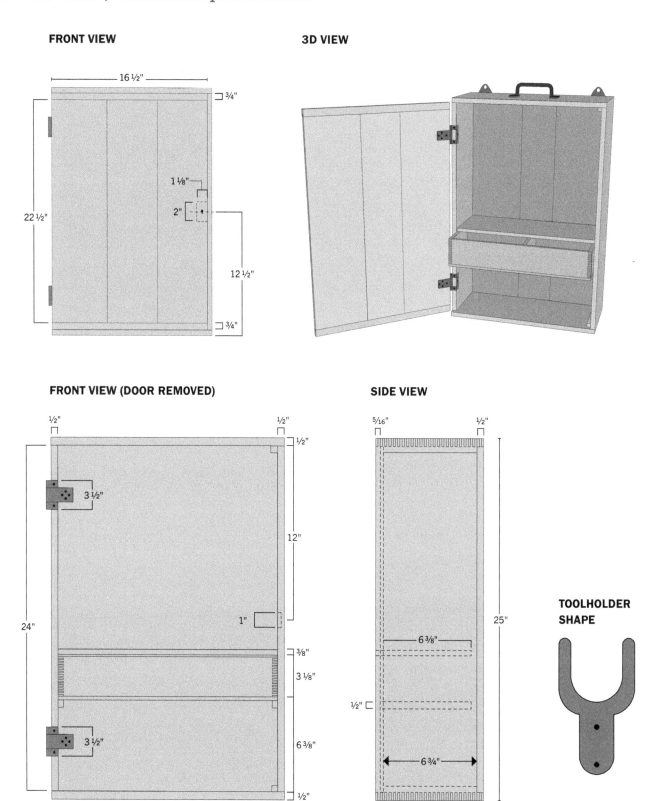

Cut a 12" length of the brass wire. Bend the middle of the brass around a metal-bending form or socket. Form a sort of M shape to make the arms. A wire jewelry bending jig or screws set into a piece of wood can be used. Using pliers, twist each arm 90° and then bend the straight section of the wire on the same form you used in the first step of this procedure. Use the tip of your needle nose pliers to form a tight circle and trim off any excess wire. Using pliers, grab each arm about ¼" from the end and bend/flare them out just a bit so it's easier to push a tool into the holder. You can further refine the fit once installed. Lay out where you want the hardware to be in the cabinet. Then, mark where the screws will go (they are all going to be a little different); use a center punch to mark the location.

You can set a countersink backward on your drill bit to form a nice consistent depth stop to avoid drilling through the wood. For narrow

## CUT LIST & MATERIALS

| | NO. | ITEM | DIMENSIONS (INCHES) | | | MATERIAL | COMMENTS |
|---|---|---|---|---|---|---|---|
| | | | T | W | L | | |
| ☐ | 1 | Left side | ½ | 7 | 24 | Eastern white pine | |
| ☐ | 1 | Right side | ½ | 7 13/16 | 24 | Eastern white pine | |
| ☐ | 2 | Top/bottom | ½ | 7 13/16 | 17 | Eastern white pine | |
| ☐ | 1 | Door | ½ | 16 ½ | 22 ½ | Eastern white pine | Trim to fit. |
| ☐ | 2 | Door breadboard ends | ¾ | ½ | 16 ½ | Eastern white pine | Trim to fit. |
| ☐ | 1 | Back | ½ | 16 ½ | 24 ½ | Eastern white pine | Floating panel |
| ☐ | 1 | Shelf | ⅜ | 6 ⅜ | 17 | Eastern white pine | Trim to fit. |
| ☐ | 2 | Drawer front/back | ½ | 3 ⅛ | 16 | Eastern white pine | |
| ☐ | 2 | Drawer sides | ⅜ | 3 ⅛ | 6 ⅜ | Eastern white pine | |
| ☐ | 1 | Drawer bottom | ¼ | 6 ⅜ | 16 | Eastern white pine | |
| ☐ | 2 | Drawer runners | 7/16 | 7/16 | 6 ⅜ | Eastern white pine | |
| ☐ | 4 | Utility hooks | | | 2 ¾ | Brass-plated steel | |
| ☐ | | Square hooks | | | ½ | Brass-plated | |
| ☐ | | Square hooks | | | 1 | Brass-plated | |
| ☐ | 2 | Overlay door hinges | | | ½ | Brass-plated | |
| ☐ | 1 | Standard-cut cupboard right lock | | | 2 | | |
| ☐ | | 8-32 hex nuts | | 11/32 | ⅛ | Brass | |
| ☐ | | #8 flat washers | | ⅜ OD | .039 | Brass | |
| ☐ | 1 | 260 sheet | 1/16 | 4 | 36 | Brass (cartridge) | |
| ☐ | 1 | 260 wire, 1 lb. spool | .064-dia. | | 83' | | |
| ☐ | 1 | Wire bending jig, such as Wire Wizard | | | | | |
| ☐ | 1 | Wire bending jig, such as Artistic Wire Deluxe | | | | | |
| ☐ | 2 | Nylon webbing strap* | | | 6 | | |

* If you have an old backpack laying around, you can repurpose the strips. Simply cut to size and cut a lighter to seal/melt the ends.

**Gather tools for wire bending.** A few simple tools are all you need to precisely bend wire for tool holders.

**Start with a U shape.** Use the corresponding groove in the wire bending jig (left). Then use the artistic wire jig to add a couple more bends (right). Go back to the wire bending jig for a second U (bottom left). Finish off with two small loops in the back, made with pliers (bottom right).

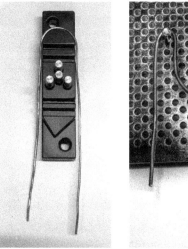

pieces, you may consider filing down the points of some of the brass screws to make them a bit shorter.

## HEAVY TOOL HOLDERS

This simple but sturdy tool holder is great for holding heavier items like hammers and larger items like your cutting gauge (see p. 41). Start with some 0.063"-thick sheet brass. Trace your template onto the brass plate with a permanent marker. Mark the center of the small mounting holes using a center punch. Use some scrap plywood to support the plate as you cut it with a jigsaw fitted with a metal cutting blade.

Place the rough-cut holder in a vise with wood jaws and use a single cut file to refine the shape of your holder; remove any burrs and round over the edges. Remember that a file only cuts on the push stroke—don't drag the file back and forth like a saw, as that will only shorten the life of the file.

Place the cut-out holder in your wood-faced vise jaws and bend it. Warm or hot brass will be more pliable. If you work quickly through the prior steps, you may have enough residual heat left in the metal, or you can heat it up a bit with an iron or a torch. It is ideal for your bend to have some spring back that leaves the arms tilted up just a bit.

Flip the piece over and place about an inch of the arms in the vice to bend the tips of the arms up a bit more to help keep tools on the hook during travel. Drill through the marks you made earlier with the punch and use a countersink bit to fit your brass screws. Install these hooks in the same manner you installed the wire tool holders.

## 3D PRINTED HARDWARE

One of the more interesting pieces of hardware in the back of this cabinet was a cast iron bit holder designed to hold tapered bits for use with a brace. This piece of hardware has not been made in almost a century, so I needed to come up with an alternate way to produce this piece. Using the original as a sample, I made a 3D model of this piece and printed it in black ABS on my 3D printer. Don't worry, if you don't have a 3D printer there are lots of online services that will print a part for you for a reasonable price or ask around, as you may have a friend with one. Print the part with 100% infill, a brim, and full support material.

The 3D printed model is made in two interlocking pieces to fit a wider range of print beds. Any support material can be removed with nippers, files, or a craft knife. Once installed, it does a great job of holding bits and from any reasonable distance it's hard to tell its not also a cast metal piece. Use three slotted brass pan head screws.

## CONCLUSION

The Sloyd tool cabinet is a nice skill builder that results in a useful object—much in the spirit of Sloyd training—and is great for taking some core tools to a workshop or jobsite around the house. You may also want to consider making one with or for someone eager to learn woodworking. As we learned from an 1898 ad for the cabinet (see "A New Tool Cabinet," p. 30), a cabinet filled with good, useful tools makes a practical holiday gift. ■

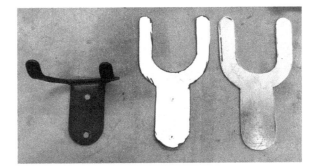

**Craft the hammer holder.** It is fashioned out of brass. Make a template and trace onto a piece of brass sheet (top). I used a jigsaw with a metal cutting blade to cut it out (center). File the edges to finish the shape (bottom).

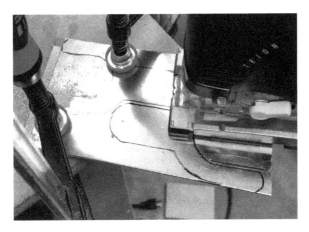

**Make the bit holder.** The original is cast iron, but I 3D-modeled it and printed it in black ABS plastic. It's printed in two pieces to fit the bed of a small 3D printer.

# TRAVELING TOOL CHEST

## Historic proportions and details are still the best.

BY CHRISTOPHER SCHWARZ

Since I started woodworking in about 1993, I've stored my tools in almost every way imaginable—from plastic buckets to wall cabinets, racks, and a variety of tool chests.

After exploring each of these methods, I kept coming back to a traditional tool chest because I have not found a better way to protect and organize my tools. I also appreciate the finite capacity of a tool chest—it forces me to think hard before buying an additional tool.

During most visits to the tool store I conclude: If it doesn't fit in the chest, I probably don't need it.

### THE RIGHT CHEST SIZE
Tool chests are built in a number of fairly standard sizes that are based on the sizes of typical tools and the limits of our bodies.

Large floor chests are usually about 24" x 24" x 40" and are designed to hold full-size saws and large jointer planes, which can be longer than 30". These chests also hold a full set of molding planes, bench planes, and all the small tools needed to make any piece of furniture. These chests are difficult to move alone, which is a disadvantage if you are by yourself, but is an advantage if someone is trying to steal your chest (the thief needs an accomplice).

Medium-size chests are just big enough to hold panel saws and smaller metal jointer planes—about 18" x 18" x 30"—and can be picked up by one person. It's an ideal size for someone who works alone, has to move the chest on occasion, and doesn't require a full set of molding planes.

This medium-size chest can hold a remarkable amount of tools—two panel saws, three backsaws, the three standard bench planes, a rabbet plane, plow plane, and router plane all fit on its floor. The two sliding trays and rack hold everything else you (should) need.

Smaller chests—the third size—were usually used for site work or by "gentlemen" woodworkers who had a small kit of tools.

The medium-size chest in this article is ideal for someone getting started in woodworking with a small shop and a budding kit of tools. It's easy to build, fairly tough, and can easily be transported to schools. When I build tool chests for

**The gang's all here.** When cutting through-dovetails, I gang-cut the tail boards to save time and effort.

**Ease the entry.** Beveling the interior corners of the tail boards makes assembly easier. And you are much less likely to damage your tails when driving them into the pins.

**Long sleeves.** Sleeve the assembled carcase over your benchtop to make it easy to level the front and back of the chest.

**Groove your bottom, then tongue it.** I use a tongue-and-groove plane to cut the joints on the long edges of the bottom boards. This plane cuts both the male and female bits.

**Tweaked.** If your carcase isn't square, clamp across the long diagonal to pull it square while you nail on the bottom boards.

**Resist rot.** Either make your rot strips impervious to water (plastic would work, too), or make them so they will rot off immediately by using pine and iron nails. Either way works.

The lid is a thick panel that is surrounded by a dust seal on three sides; the seal pieces are dovetailed at the corners because this area of a tool chest takes heaps of abuse.

Most of the carcase is made from a lightweight and inexpensive wood such as pine. The parts that will see heavy wear are oak. We'll discuss the interior fittings after we get the carcase complete.

### MAKE THE SHELL

Join the corners of the carcase with through-dovetails—six dovetails at each corner are suitable for a chest this size. Smooth the inside faces of the boards and assemble the carcase. Once the glue is dry, level the joints and remove the tool marks from the case's exterior.

Fetch the pine bottom boards. The grain should run from front to back in the chest (for strength), and the long edges of the boards should have some sort of joint to accommodate wood movement. I used the tongue-and-groove joint. Then I cut a ³/₁₆" bead on the tongue boards as decoration.

Attach the bottom boards to the carcase with 6d headed nails—I used cut clouts. Be sure to leave some room between the boards for expansion and contraction. Trim the bottom boards flush with the carcase.

The last bit on the shell is to attach the rot strips to the underside of the bottom boards. I use water-resistant white oak and attach it to the bottom with waterproof glue and brass screws. After finishing, I oil and wax these rot strips to make them repel water.

customers, this is far and away the most requested size.

### HOW IT'S BUILT

The carcase is dovetailed together—the strongest joint available. The bottom boards are, however, nailed onto the carcase so they are easily replaced if they rot. Speaking of rot, the entire chest sits on two oak "rot strips" screwed to the bottom boards, keeping the chest off a wet floor.

The bottom and top skirts on this chest are mitered and nailed to the carcase. I typically dovetail the skirts at the corners, but a well-made miter can survive just fine.

**FRONT VIEW**

**SIDE VIEW**

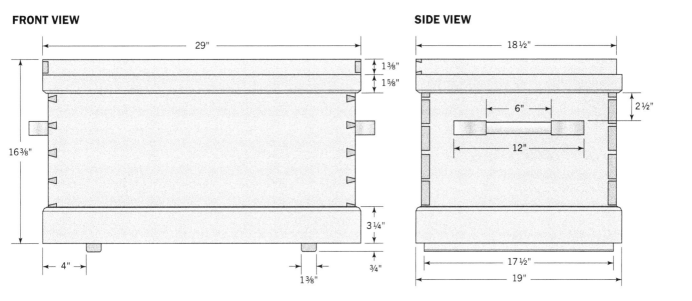

**INTERIOR FITTINGS**

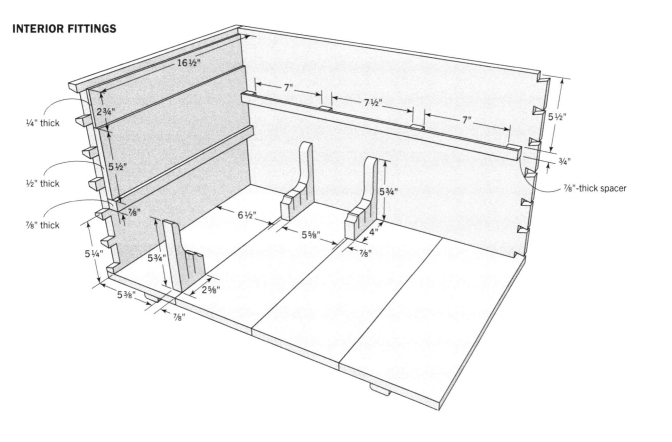

**Completely stuck.** Mold the entire stick of wood before cutting it apart for mitering. This ensures the molding will match at the corners.

## MITERED SKIRTING

The bottom skirt protects the carcase from kicks and bumps. The top skirt helps seal the interior from dust and protects the lid's dust seal. The skirting is ½"-thick stuff that wraps around the entire carcase and is mitered at the corners.

Before cutting the miters, however, cut any molding or bevels. These are not just decorative—a 90° corner is fragile and will quickly splinter off in the shop. I used a ⅜" square ovolo on the bottom skirt. The top skirt has a ⅛" bead on its top edge and a 30° bevel on the bottom edge.

Now attach the skirting to the carcase. I miter molding with a miter box, which I find more accurate than power equipment. All the miters here were assembled right from the saw. That's not because I'm awesome; it's because a miter box allows you to put a sawtooth right on a knife line.

Glue and nail the skirting to the carcase—don't forget to apply glue to the miters themselves. Then clamp the corners while the glue dries. At this point I would typically work on the lid and its dust seal. But because

Jameel Abraham was working on the lid panel, I fitted out the interior with trays, saw tills, and a rack.

## THE INTERIOR

The arrangement shown in this chest is typical and works well. On the floor of the chest are two small saw tills—one for backsaws and the other for two panel saws. I like these tills because they take up little space.

Floating above the floor are two sliding trays—one deep and one shallow. The deep tray is for bulky tools such as the brace and bit, plus anything in a tool roll. The top tray is for all the small tools you use every day—layout tools, block plane, mallet, hammer, and wax, for example.

The tray walls are made from pine. The bottoms and the runners they slide on are oak to resist wear.

On the back wall of the chest is a rack for holding small or handled tools—chisels, dividers, combination squares, and screwdrivers.

## INSTALL THE RUNNERS

The sliding trays run on oak runners that are affixed to the inside of the

**Miters all around.** I begin mitering at one front corner of the chest. I get that joint perfect, then I make my way around the carcase.

**Yes, clamp.** Glue the short grain of each miter and clamp it at the corners. The glue will have more strength this way.

carcase. There are three layers of runners for the two trays, all of different thicknesses and widths so the trays can be pulled up and out.

The lowest runners are installed 5 1/4" from the floor of the chest—that gives your bench planes the headroom they need. I install these lower runners by first making a spacer board from some scrap that is 5 1/4" wide (see below left photo). I use that as a temporary shelf to hold the lower runners in position while I glue and nail them.

After the lower runners are installed, remove the spacer and install the runners above, also with nails and glue. I cut a small bead on the top edge of each to protect the corner from damage and to spruce up the interior a bit.

## BUILD THE TRAYS

The trays are dovetailed at the corners and each has a thin oak bottom that is nailed on. The interesting detail here is that the finished trays are 1/8" smaller than the bottoms are long. In other words, the bottoms are

1/16" proud on either end of the assembled trays.

This detail makes the trays easy to fit. You only have to get the bottoms to slide smoothly on the runners. The trays never touch the runners or interfere with the sliding action. Fit the bottom boards so they are a close but smooth fit on the runners.

**3D VIEW: TRAYS**

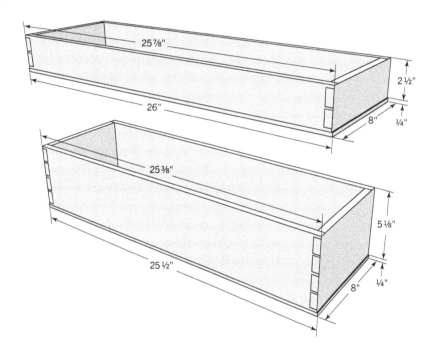

**This high.** The 5 1/4"-wide spacer acts as a shelf when installing the runner above it. The 5 1/4" height is critical for holding standard bench planes below the bottom tray.

**Smooth-sliding bottom.** The bottom boards are the only part that touches the runners. So shoot them to perfect length until you get the sliding action you want with zero racking.

**Proud bottom.** Here you can see how the bottom protrudes from the end of the tray, making the tray a cinch to fit.

**Rack at the back.** This simple rack (left) can hold a variety of tools (right). My other favorite form of rack is a board that is poked with ½"-diameter holes on 1 ⅛" centers.

 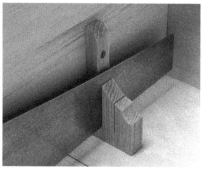

**Quick saw till.** Kerf the block of wood for the saws, then shape the block so it looks nice (left). Screw it to the side of the carcase and to a bottom board (right).

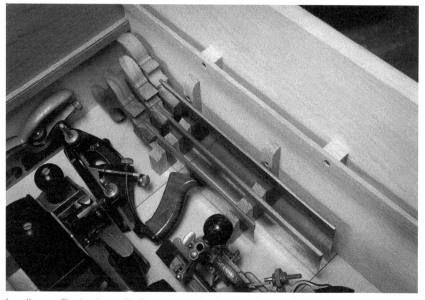

**Loading up.** The backsaw till offers more protection than the panel-saw till because backsaws are more fragile.

Now dovetail and assemble the trays. Then nail or screw the bottoms on. If you need to use multiple boards for the bottoms, shiplap the joints at their mating edges.

### RACKS AND TILLS

I like simple racks and tills for my chests because that leaves more room to arrange the tools. The rack on the back wall is made from scrap bits of oak that I glued together, then screwed onto the back wall with #8 x 1¼" screws.

The saw till for the panel saws is simply one piece of oak with two kerfs cut into it. One kerf is for the crosscut saw and the second is for the rip saw. This till holds the saws at their tips. The weight of the handle and the teeth at the heel of the saw prevents the tools from whipping around in the chest.

The till for the backsaws is made and attached in the same manner. The only difference is that there are two blocks of wood and three kerfs in each for the dovetail, carcase, and tenon saw. This till is at the back of the chest.

### CHEST LIFTS

While you should carry your chest by holding its bottom (or put it on a cart), the lifts help you get the chest into position or to balance your load. Each lift is made from a single piece of oak that looks like a dog's bone when you begin. You turn down the center to make a handle. Then shape the ends of the "bone" to make them look nice. I used a simple ogee curve.

The proper way to attach the lifts is to screw them in place from both the outside and the inside of the chest. The #8 screws from the outside pass through the narrow ends of the lifts. The screws from the inside are driven into the thick part near the handle.

## THE LID

If you are skipping the embellished panel, make the lid from a softwood that doesn't move much, such as one of the white pines. Glue it up from several pieces of quartersawn or rift-sawn stock to further reduce seasonal movement.

After cutting the panel to size—it's a bit larger than the rim of the carcase—attach it to the carcase with hinges. With the lid in its final position, you then can build the dust seal around it to create a perfect fit.

After building about 20 of these chests, I have found a better way to make the dust seal fit. I rabbet each piece until that piece fits perfectly flush with the top skirt and the top edge of the lid. I can adjust this fit in tiny increments with a shoulder plane.

Then, once all three pieces of the dust seal fit perfectly, I dovetail them together at the corners.

I attach the seal using a combination of glue and nails. Glue and nail the front edge of the dust seal to the lid. To attach the "returns" along the ends of the chest, use glue and nails along the front 4" of the lid. Then use nails alone for the rest. This fastening method allows the top to move.

To keep the chest secure, I installed a traditional crab lock—a blacksmith-made lock built for chests that allows for some wood movement. They are easy to install because they are surface-mounted to

**Turn the bone.** The center section of the dog bone is turned down to 1" diameter. Then remove the piece from the lathe.

**Rasp the bone.** Then shape the ends of the lifts. This shape leaves plenty of meat for the screws to bite into.

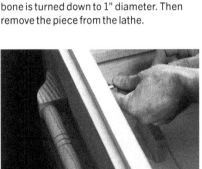

**Screwed either way.** Affix the lifts with stout #8 screws from both the inside and outside of the carcase.

**Rabbet the seal.** The rabbet on this piece of the dust seal allows you to sneak up on the perfect fit all around.

**Rabbeted dovetails.** This joinery looks a little involved, but it's actually simple. Begin by cutting a tail on the seal, then show it to its mate. You'll then know what to do.

**Keyholed.** The only tough part about installing a crab lock is cutting a well-placed and crisp keyhole. I bored the hole for the round part of the key. Then I cut the remainder with a chisel.

the inside of the chest. And they are gorgeous.

## THE BEST FINISH

Almost all traditional tool chests were painted. It is the most durable and easy-to-renew finish. You can use any paint you like—milk paint, oil paint, or latex. Paint the outside of the chest, but leave the inside of the chest bare—or use a coat of wax alone if you like.

If you insist on a film finish for the inside, use shellac. Please avoid oils—they will stink forever.

Once your chest is complete, my final caution is to avoid bringing it into your house. Many chests like this begin their lives intending to hold tools but somehow end up at the foot of the bed stuffed with blankets and doilies. A sad situation, indeed. ■

## CUT LIST & MATERIALS

| | NO. | ITEM | DIMENSIONS (INCHES) | | | MATERIAL |
|---|---|---|---|---|---|---|
| | | | T | W | L | |
| **CARCASE** | | | | | | |
| □ | 2 | Front/back | 3/4 | 14 7/8 | 28 | Pine |
| □ | 2 | Ends | 3/4 | 14 7/8 | 18 | Pine |
| □ | 1 | Bottom* | 5/8 | 28 | 18 | Pine |
| □ | 2 | Rot strips | 3/4 | 1 3/8 | 17 1/2 | White oak |
| □ | 2 | Bottom skirt, front/back | 1/2 | 3 1/4 | 29 | Pine |
| □ | 2 | Bottom skirt, ends | 1/2 | 3 1/4 | 19 | Pine |
| □ | 2 | Top skirt, front/back | 1/2 | 1 5/8 | 29 | Pine |
| □ | 2 | Top skirt, ends | 1/2 | 1 5/8 | 19 | Pine |
| □ | 2 | Chest lifts | 1 1/4 | 1 3/4 | 12 | Oak |
| □ | 1 | Lid panel | 7/8 | 18 1/16 | 28 3/8 | Pine† |
| □ | 1 | Dust seal, front | 1/2 | 1 1/2‡ | 29 | Pine |
| □ | 2 | Dust seal, ends | 1/2 | 1 1/2‡ | 19‡ | Pine |
| **INTERIOR FITTINGS** | | | | | | |
| □ | 2 | Bottom runners | 7/8 | 7/8 | 16 1/2 | Oak |
| □ | 2 | Middle runners | 1/2 | 5 1/2 | 16 1/2 | Oak |
| □ | 2 | Top runners | 1/4 | 2 3/4 | 16 1/2 | Oak |
| **BOTTOM TRAY** | | | | | | |
| □ | 2 | Front/back | 1/2 | 5 1/8 | 25 3/8 | Pine |
| □ | 2 | Ends | 1/2 | 5 1/8 | 8 | Pine |
| □ | 1 | Bottom | 1/4 | 8 | 25 1/2 | Oak |
| **TOP TRAY** | | | | | | |
| □ | 2 | Front/back | 1/2 | 2 1/2 | 25 7/8 | Pine |
| □ | 2 | Ends | 1/2 | 2 1/2 | 8 | Pine |
| □ | 1 | Bottom | 1/4 | 8 | 26 | Oak |
| **TOOL HOLDERS** | | | | | | |
| □ | 1 | Panel-saw till | 7/8 | 2 5/8 | 5 3/4 | Oak |
| □ | 2 | Backsaw tills | 7/8 | 4 | 5 3/4 | Oak |
| □ | 1 | Rack, front piece | 1/4 | 3/4 | 25 1/2 | Oak |
| □ | 4 | Rack spacers | 5/8 | 3/4 | 1 | Oak |
| **SUPPLIES** | | | | | | |
| □ | 2 | Chest hinges | | | | |
| □ | 1 | Crab lock | | | | |

* Made from multiple boards. † Plywood if making an embellished lid (for more information, see www.popularwoodworking.com/article/tool-chest-as-art). ‡ Dust seal measurements are slightly oversized to allow a custom fit.

# ONE FOR THE ROAD

**This cabinetmaker's tool chest is ready to travel.**

BY TOM FIDGEN

**W**hen I think of a tool chest, I think of a carpenter's box, usually open and inviting, a little rough, perhaps, but clearly made by the hand. Think of Roy Underhill merrily skipping over the stream—remember the toolbox he was carrying? What I've come up with is a toolbox, made entirely by hand, that is both practical and traditional in construction. Well, sort of.

Do you need to carry tools? Are you going to be on a jobsite outside of your workshop? This chest will be manageable and hold most of your

**A tale of tails.** This is a typical dovetail layout—but for visual interest, I simply refrained from cutting out the center tail.

**A bit of choice.** You can use a bit and brace to remove the majority of the waste in a dado.

workshop essentials while incorporating some unique and practical design elements.

For starters, the sliding lid (captured in dados) pushes off the back and is held open to access the interior. While in the open position, the lid serves as a shield to cover two backsaws that are safely held on the exterior back with a protective shelf underneath them. This turns into a little shelf to place things like tiny screws you'd surely lose on-site if you didn't have such a dedicated area to toss them into.

It has a built-in shooting board, and a workspace complete with surface clamp and miter hook that will get all of the applause from your fellow craftsmen. I don't know how many times I've been installing a cabinet or perhaps some finish molding somewhere, and a makeshift bench surface, saw hook, and shooting board would have been really handy—it's also nice to rest your arse on the edge from time to time. It's simple in form, as a tool chest should

be. We'll get started with the basic box so we can get on to some of those unique design elements.

**THE CARCASE**

Whether you're using four wide planks or joining up some narrower widths, assemble the four main carcase components after working up your cutting list from the illustrations (yes, it's an important part of the process!). Those pieces are the front, back, and the two ends, or sides, if you will.

The front corner joinery will be through-dovetails; the back has a tenons housed in stopped dados. The sides will continue past the chest back, creating a kind of shelf location where two backsaws will live. Follow your through-dovetail procedure and lay out, cut, and dry fit the front to the side pieces.

To create this "staggered" or "broken" dovetail pattern, I laid out the entire width of the pieces as per normal, then simply refrained from cutting out the center tail after marking.

**Clean up.** A router plane completes the dado and cleans up the bottom.

**Magic lid.** A rotating connector, or roto hinge, will hold the top lid in place and allow it to travel freely (left), holding it in place again at the back while in the open position. Once the lid travels past the back panel, it'll swing down to rest in the vertical position (right).

## CUT LIST & MATERIALS

| | NO. | ITEM | DIMENSIONS (INCHES) | | | MATERIAL | COMMENTS |
|---|---|---|---|---|---|---|---|
| | | | T | W | L | | |
| ☐ | 1 | Back panel | 3/4 | 8 5/8 | 19 | Hard maple | |
| ☐ | 1 | Front panel | 3/4 | 8 5/8 | 20 1/2 | Hard maple | |
| ☐ | 2 | Side panels | 3/4 | 9 3/8 | 9 1/2 | Hard maple | |
| ☐ | 4 | Top/bottom caps | 1 | 1 | 9 1/2 | Walnut | In dados in ends. |
| ☐ | 1 | Back stretcher | 3/4 | 1 7/8 | 20 1/2 | Hard maple | |
| ☐ | 1 | Lid | 3/4 | 6 3/4 | 19 | Hard maple | |
| ☐ | 2 | Till cleats | 3/4 | 7/8 | 5 1/4 | Hard maple | |
| ☐ | 1 | Wide bottom panel | 1/4 | 5 5/8 | 19 1/2 | Hard maple | |
| ☐ | 1 | Thin bottom panel | 1/4 | 2 3/8 | 19 1/2 | Hard maple | |
| ☐ | 2 | Till ends | 1/2 | 1 5/16 | 5 1/8 | Poplar | |
| ☐ | 2 | Till sides | 1/2 | 2 11/16 | 18 3/8 | Poplar | |
| ☐ | 1 | Till bottom | 1/2 | 4 5/8 | 16 7/8 | Walnut | |
| ☐ | 2 | Till handles | 1/2-dia. | | 4 5/8 | Walnut dowels | |
| ☐ | 1 | Top handle | 1/2 | 1 3/8 | 23 3/8 | Walnut | |
| ☐ | 2 | Handle supports | 3/4 | 2 3/16 | 14 1/8 | Walnut | |
| ☐ | 1 | Shooting board base | 1/2 | 4 | 18 1/4 | Hard maple | |
| ☐ | 1 | Shooting board stop | 3/4 | 3/4 | 4 | Walnut | |
| ☐ | 2 | Roto hinges | | | | | |
| ☐ | | Tenon reinforcement | | | | Dowels | Cut to fit. |
| ☐ | 2 | Backsaw holder cleats | 1/2 | 1 3/8 | 23 3/8 | Scrap maple | |
| ☐ | | Rare earth magnets | | | | | |
| ☐ | 1 | Small shelf for vertical workholding | | | | Scrap maple | |
| ☐ | 2 | Cam clamps | | | | | |
| ☐ | 1 | Surface clamp | | | | | |

**Dado work ahead.** You can see the lid stops at this point; I will disassemble the tool chest and lengthen the 'L' shaped dado so, when open, the lid will be flush with the top of the sides.

**Till parts.** Till components are cut with the ends already dovetailed.

When you scribe the tail board over to the pins, it'll be business as usual. This break creates some visual interest and actually saves you time in construction! If all is well in dovetail land, we can disassemble, mark, and scribe the interior dado to house the back-panel tenon.

Once I have the bulk of the waste removed, I like to use my Japanese dozuki to establish the depth of the dado (yes, I said pull saw—this is one application where a Western-style saw would not be appropriate) by laying the saw plate in the narrow shoulder of the stopped dado and drawing the saw back toward me. Again, this is just something I like to do to help with tear out and could easily be accomplished with a wide chisel.

Once you get close to your finished depth, remove the rest of material with the mortise chisel. Clean up the bottom with the router plane and call it done. In the outside edges of the toolbox back, cut a corresponding tongue or tenon with either a skew block plane or rabbet plane. Another dry fit, and we'll cut the stopped dados for the bottom panels.

Because we're using through-dovetails here, the bottom dado needs to be stopped so it doesn't show up in the outside end grain. You could let it (this being a toolbox), but I'm going to take the extra steps to cut stopped dados. Lay out the dado and, starting at one corner, chop out the waste by hand. This will give the end of your plow plane somewhere to go when beginning. Now with my plow plane, I can safely cut the dado.

I purchased these roto hinges years ago for a project and they were sold in a bag of six. I figured they'd come in handy someday, and this lid design is the perfect application. Make sure the dado is deep enough to let the hinge travel its full distance. Cut the lid to size and drill the corresponding holes. A dry fit and test run will be next.

**INTERIOR COMPONENTS**
Before I disassemble, I'll measure, cut, and fit the interior cleats that will hold the till inside. This is also a good time to double-check the size of the bottom panel and mark out the dovetail for the back stretcher.

Assemble the pieces needed for the till. I used some poplar, and this

**CROSS SECTION**

**EXPLODED VIEW**

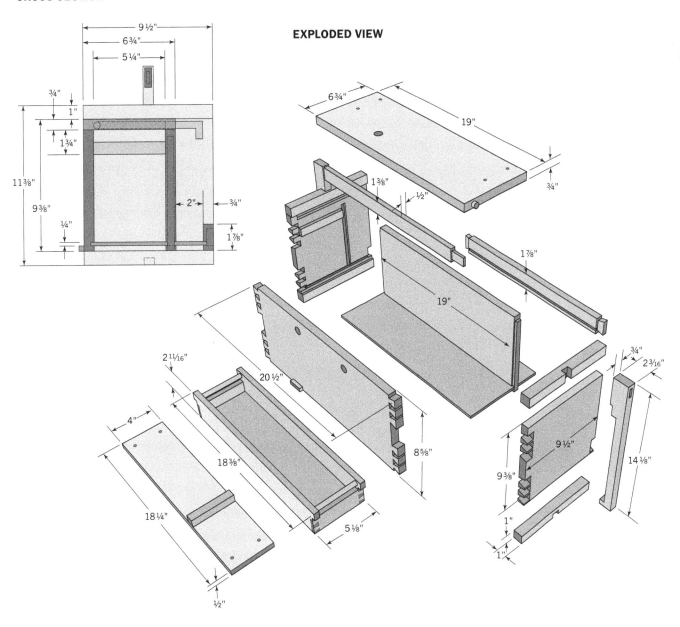

lightweight wood will help to keep the toolbox lighter. Cut the two side pieces to length, then measure and cut out the shoulders that will hang off the interior cleats. A nice snug fit here is what we're after. It'll be dovetailed shortly and when we trim the tails, it will be shortened ever-so-slightly for a perfect fit.

I'm using through-dovetails for the till, but didn't want to go through the trouble of cutting stopped dados for the bottom. This is kind of a neat method for through-dovetail construction without having to go through the steps of stopped dados.

Assemble the till components. The two long sides are already cut to fit; now cut the two ends to size as well. Begin on the ends with laying out and cutting the tails as you normally would do for any dovetail.

The next step is where this method differs from usual. Take the two short ends and cut the groove for the till bottom. Now before we go ahead and scribe the thickness of the ends

**Ready to move on.** The end pieces are now ready for the next step.

**Ready for assembly.** The frame components are now ready for assembly.

onto the two long pieces, we'll rip the sides off at the tails at the same depth as the newly cut dado, creating a thinner version.

Next, with our tails ripped and crosscut to width and the waste removed, we can go ahead and transfer this new thickness to the long sides of the till. Once scribed we'll transfer the tails over to the pin board using our usual methods.

With the tails scribed, cut out the pins. Now we don't have to worry about the dados showing on the outside of the till. Cut the dado to the full length of the front and back till components.

Measure and cut the till's bottom panel. It's also a good time to round over the top edges of the till sides and drill for the dowels which get set into the inside ends. These will act as handles and will make it much easier to pick the full till up from inside the tool chest. A dry fit and we're ready to glue. I didn't put any finish on mine, deciding to leave it in its natural state.

With the interior components completed I'll measure, mark and cut out the dovetails for the back bottom stretcher.

This piece is also rabbetted using the same "no-stop rabbet" method of cutting the tail. Plow out the bottom-panel groove then rip the tail to width, essentially cutting off the groove's shoulders. Scribe the tail to the side panels and cut the sockets. I decided to add a decorative bead to the stretcher as well as the top and bottom of the front panel.

Measure and cut the bottom panels and give everything another good going over. With that, it'll be time to spread some glue.

### EXTERIOR FRAME AND HANDLE

I used some walnut offcuts and built a kind of cradle that will capture the ends and transfer the weight through the handle, down the sides, and underneath to help pick up some of the weight of the finished toolbox.

With two bottom caps/runners cut to length, I'll cut and chisel a small open mortise that will house the stub tenon at the bottom of the two side uprights. This will be glued and screwed using some cast bronze screws left over from my boat-building days. This type of hardware is great for any application that may see moisture, such as the bottom of a tool chest.

When all of the handle joinery is to your liking, disassemble and give everything a good going over with a smoothing plane. Glue and re-assemble. When the glue is dry, I'll drill and install some dowels through the tenons and runners to lock everything in place for good.

### BACKSAW HOLDERS

The backsaw holders are cut from maple scraps. I used my bowsaw to shape them and some file and rasp work to finish. These will be screwed to the back along with a small block holding two inset rare earth magnets. The backsaws simply fit over the custom-shaped cleats and grab the magnets, which holds everything in place for our adventures on down the road.

### ON-SITE CLAMPING

When we get to our destination, we need to hold our work. Anyone who's been at a client's home trying to saw a board or dress an edge on

**Trace (left).** Here, I'm shaping one of two cleats that will become back saw holders. These were simply traced from my hand saws and cut out.

**Field jointing (right).** With the surface clamp in one of the front holes and a ¾" dowel in the other, I can edge joint a board up to 24" long!

their kitchen counter or coffee table will know this is awkward to say the least. We'll make some custom benchtop appliances suited for this scale of work.

Once at our jobsite, the first thing you'll do is clamp the tool chest to a table or countertop. This is done with our two wooden cam clamps that will live in front of the backsaws on our rear panel. A couple of little blocks glued in place will be plenty enough to hold them while en route.

Now onto the lid and front. Drill a few ¾" holes in your nice new toolbox. Don't worry, these will turn this pretty little tool chest into an on-site tabletop workbench! The front two holes are used in conjunction with a surface clamp, bench dog, or simply a wooden dowel.

For vertical workholding applications, I also cut and shaped a little shelf or lip that provides somewhere for the end of a board to sit while clamped to the front panel. This small maple shelf receives a rabbet and is then glued and screwed.

On-site edge jointing? Again, no worries. Clamp your workpiece horizontally into the left-side hole and rest the opposite end on a bench dog or dowel installed in the right side. This is why we clamped our box down when we began.

What's that? An on-the-job shooting board attachment? Cool. Measure, cut, and square up a thin piece of stock suitable for a shooting board. Drill and glue four dowels into the bottom corners; when the glue is dry, cut them so they're in the ¼" ballpark. Drill four corresponding holes into the top of the lid, giving these a nice countersink. The lid serves as the plane track.

The fence is screwed in place, up from the bottom; make sure it's perfectly square to the ramp side. When you're not using the board, it can stay put there on top; when you need the surface lid space for other work-holding needs, it can be stored on the back shelf in front of the backsaws.

A mixture of oil and varnish for the outside and we can call this project done. Congratulations! You now have somewhere to keep your essential, on-site hand tools, as well as a great little workbench for out-of-shop work. ■

# TRAVELING TOOLBOX

**Bodger and blacksmith Don Weber shows how to effectively combine power- and hand-tool techniques to build a simple and sturdy toolbox.**

BY DON WEBER

I'm a bodger and a blacksmith, making tables and chairs in iron and wood. When I'm not in the shop, I'm journeying to woodworking shows to demonstrate the spring pole lathe or teach workshops in traditional woodworking and metal smithing. I travel quite a bit, and if you've ever watched the way the baggage handlers deal with your luggage, you'll understand why I built an oak box banded in iron to carry my woodworking tools.

The toolbox described here was made of quartersawn oak from a winery in northern California. I've built instrument cases for rare and antique musical instruments, and I've found the lids moved considerably with humidity changes. So with this toolbox, I've allowed the top and bottom to float in a groove in the sides and ends, much like a frame-and-panel door.

I had the oak boards resawn to ½" thick. All the joinery was done on a table saw with the help of a rebate plane (here in America we call a "rebate" a "rabbet," but I prefer the traditional English term), a Stanley No. 5 (jack plane), and a low-angle block plane. I reinforced the corners

**Joint the edges.** I use my jack plane to joint the edges of the side boards. The plane's iron is slightly cambered across its width to allow me to correct an out-of-square edge.

**Glue up.** When gluing up a panel, I rub the glue joint up and down to ensure a gap-free joint.

**Clamp it.** A couple of clamps across the joint are good insurance—even if you have a good edge joint. The cauls keep the panel flat.

### CUT LIST & MATERIALS

| | NO. | ITEM | DIMENSIONS (INCHES) | | | MATERIAL |
|---|---|---|---|---|---|---|
| | | | T | W | L | |
| ☐ | 2 | Top/bottom | ½ | 13 ¾ | 30 ¼ | Oak |
| ☐ | 2 | Ends | ¾ | 8 | 14 | Oak |
| ☐ | 2 | Sides | ¾ | 8 | 31 | Oak |
| ☐ | 2 | Hinges | | | | |
| ☐ | 2 | Handles | | | | |
| ☐ | | Pins | ⅛-dia. | | | Locust |
| ☐ | 2 | Ledger | ½ | ½ | 14 | Oak |

of the box with ⅛"-diameter locust pins because I forged corner brackets (not shown here) as well as the hinges, latch and handles. (I've been influenced by the Tansu hardware of Japanese chests.)

**EDGE JOINTING BY HAND**

The top and bottom panels were made by gluing up two boards edge-to-edge. I prepare the edge for gluing with my jack plane (Mr. Jack, I call him). Cabinetmakers of old would use a longer jointer plane, but a board of this length can be accurately planed with the shorter jack. Use your fingers as a fence along the face of the board as you plane each edge. Check your results with a try square.

If you've done a good job with the plane, you should be able to create what we call a "rubbed" joint. This is where you glue each edge and rub the mating edges together until the glue begins to set up. A clamp or two is a good idea while the glue cures.

**REBATES BY HAND AND POWER**

I cut the rebates on the side pieces by first defining the joint's shoulder with my table saw and then reducing the thickness of the tongue with my rebate plane, a vintage Record No. 778. Set the height of the table saw's blade to half the thickness of the stock of the sides and ends, which is ⅜" in this case. Set the rip fence so your rebate will be ¾" wide. Cut the shoulder on the ends of the sides. Reduce the thickness of the joint with your rebate plane as shown (p. 61, top left).

For those purists out there, you can cut the rebate entirely with a rebate plane (or a Stanley No. 10, a

**Angle.** Start the plane at an angle as shown. After each pass bring the tool a bit more level. This makes a square joint.

**Chamfer.** Chamfering the edges of the top and the raised panel with a block plane softens the look.

carriagemaker's bench plane). Just be sure to use the plane's side nickers to score across the grain to prevent your grain from tearing out as you cut the joint.

The edges of the top and bottom panel were rebated all around in the same manner to fit in the groove cut in the sides and ends of the box. I set the raised portion of the panels so they are flush with the top and bottom edges of the sides. Note that the rebates on the ends of the panel are ⅜" wide. The rebate on the long edges is a different width, ¼". This arrangement allows the panel to expand across its width but not along its length. And that is proper cabinet-making.

A small chamfer is planed around the inner sides of the box frame, and the raised portion of the top and bottom, to create a visual break when the panel moves with humidity variation.

### PLOWING THE GROOVES

The top and bottom panels are fit into the grooves in the sides and ends. You could cut this groove using your table saw. But if you have a plow plane, this is the place to put it to use.

The plow plane is designed to cut grooves of different widths, which are varied by changing the cutter in the tool. The location of the groove is determined by the tool's fence, which bears against the edge of the work during the cut. The depth of the groove is determined by the tool's depth stop. Once the joint reaches its final depth, the tool will then cease to cut.

### GLUE, DRILL, AND PEG

Glue and clamp the ends to the sides with the top and bottom panels in place. Be careful not to get glue in the groove or the panel can't expand and contract as it needs to. When the glue has cured, drill ⅛"-diameter holes

**Bore holes.** Here I'm using a hand drill (sometimes called an eggbeater drill) to bore the pilot holes for my locust pins.

in the corner joints to accept the ⅛" locust pins.

The top is cut away from the glued-up box 1½" from the top edge, using a table saw. After the first two cuts are made, wedges are inserted in the slots to keep the saw blade from binding. A few pieces of masking tape keep the wedges in place.

With the saw cut complete, clean up the tooling marks on the top and bottom using a plane, scraper, or (my favorite) a small scraping plane.

The hardware for my box was hand forged in my blacksmith's shop, though there is some decent hand-wrought hardware out there. To fas-

**Make the lid.** Carefully part the lid on the table saw with wedges to hold the kerf open (left). Once the lid has been parted from the bottom, plane or scrape the sawn edges of the toolbox to remove the tooling marks (right).

ten the handles to the box, I added a ½" x ½" ledger to the inside of the box to strengthen the attachment of the handles as well as to provide a ledge for a tray for small tools.

All surfaces were dressed with a cabinet scraper and finished with an oil varnish (one pint marine spar varnish, one pint boiled linseed oil, and enough gum turpentine to thin to the consistency of half-and-half).

Once rubbed up with a scouring pad and some wax, the job is done. I have done a lot of traveling with this toolbox, inevitably filling it with more tools than it should carry, and it is still doing its job admirably. ■

## HAND-FORGED HARDWARE

I hand-forged the hardware you see here in my blacksmith shop. You could find a local blacksmithing workshop or purchase reproduction hardware for your toolbox (see Manufacturers listings).

**TOP VIEW**

**CROSS SECTION**

**LONG CROSS SECTION**

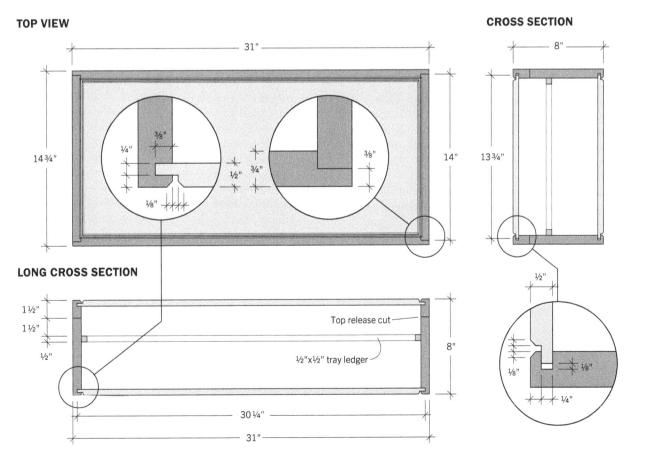

**2**

# CHESTS

**Sturdy chests you can park on your bench or shop floor. While some of these chests can travel, the larger sizes or lack of handles also make them perfect for settling more permanently on a corner of your workbench or near the action in your shop. Drawers, trays, and compartments aplenty are a common feature in this section. Helpful rules and guidelines will guide the construction of your tool chest into a detailed and thoughtfully organized workshop partner.**

# MACHINIST'S TOOL CHEST

**A few design modifications turn this garage staple into a great tool chest.**

BY ZACHARY DILLINGER

A few years ago, I found a dusty, beat-up, three-drawer machinist's toolbox in the basement of my 1900-built farmhouse. Originally made by noted tool manufacturer C.E. Jennings & Co., it had been modified several times and wasn't in very good condition. After cleaning out the contents, I've used the box to store numerous things over the years, most recently my collection of files, rasps, and various other small tools. It's been a valued part of the way I work but it had some limitations that made it less than perfect for a woodworker.

I decided to build a slightly modified version of the chest to address those limitations. The biggest changes are that it has two drawers instead of three, and I made the top well deeper. These changes allow me to store saws, planes, and chisels in the box, something that was difficult to do in the original.

## DOWEL JOINERY

The original box is built from chestnut and finished with a dark stain. When studying the original, I was unable to intuit much about the way the case of the box was constructed. No joinery is visible from the outside. Given that this early 20th century box was produced in a factory, I posit that the box was either splined or doweled together. Due to the ease of doweled construction in a hand-tool-only shop, I chose this method.

The construction begins by laying out and cutting the parts to the dimensions listed in the cutting list. To hold the case together, I used ¼" dowels, two at each of the top corners and three in each of the bottom corners. I like to use a marking gauge to lay out the drilled holes in each piece. There are dowel center points available commercially, but I personally get much better results if I lay out each hole with scribed lines and carefully drill them.

Test fit the two side frames together without glue and make any necessary adjustments. Once that's

**I ripped all of the parts for this project by hand.** Ripping with a handsaw isn't much fun but is a foundational skill. In some cases, I'll knock down stock with a hatchet to move things along quickly before approaching my line with a plane.

**Cut the rabbets.** Cutting the side panel rabbets depends as much on layout as it does skill with the cutting tools.

**Plane.** Once the side frames are together, plane the outsides flush.

**Install corner brackets.** They were steel on the original, but I opted for brass.

**Pilot-drill strips.** Install ledger strips that will support the well bottom. Once these are in place, you can add the brass brackets for the top of the box.

**Install the well bottom.** It fits under the corner brackets and sits on the ledger strips.

the clamps. Aim for a gap-free fit on the vertical pieces and rely on the top and bottom edges to hold the panel in place.

The two front pieces are constructed in exactly the same fashion as the side pieces. Crosscut and plane them to precise length, then dowel them in place. Dry fit the joinery, using a clamp to draw it all together, and make any necessary adjustments to ensure two square sides with gap-free corners. When that is finished, glue up a board wide enough for the case back and carefully fit it into the dry-assembled frame. Once you're happy with the fit, dowel it into place with four ¼" dowels (one at each corner). With all the corners fit to your specification, glue up the case.

### CASE BRACES

After an hour or so in the clamps, install the four bottom corner braces on the inside of the case. This is somewhat of an unusual technique, but the original has them. The original had steel braces but I chose to spend the little bit of extra money to go with brass to match the other hardware.

The top corners will also get these brackets, but they must wait until the top well's bottom board is in place. The next step is to make ½" square strips that will support the well bottom from below. These are screwed into place with 1" long #6 wood screws. To make sure that each strip is installed squarely, I butted each strip against the end of a combination square rule set to the proper depth, with the fence resting on the top edge. Be sure to pilot-drill each strip, as the wood screws are highly likely to split otherwise.

done, lay out and cut the ½" deep x ⅜" wide rabbets in each of the two top and bottom pieces that make up the two side frames. Then, glue and clamp up the side frames and set them aside to dry. The side panels will simply float in the rabbet and will later be held in place with the drawer runners, so you can make the panels and fit them while the frames are still in

**Postition the drawer runner.** Use ¾" scrap to precisely mark out the drawer runner length.

**Position the runner.** Use a piece of sandpaper to ensure that the runner is just slightly higher than the bottom case inside rail. This prevents hangups when fitting the drawer.

With the strips in place, cut a piece of ¼" plywood to fit the opening and plane it so that it just drops in and rests on the strips. Once you're happy with that fit, attach the top corner brackets so that the brackets hold the bottom tightly down onto the strips below. It can be a bit finicky to get the screws installed due to the limited clearance but it's possible if you pre-drill screw holes of the proper size and take your time.

## DRAWER RUNNERS

The drawer runner that supports the top drawer actually performs four separate duties. In addition to providing the running surface for the top drawer, the runners serve as drawer stops; they help hold the side panels in place; and they will ultimately hold the screws that attach the side handles. They're made from ¾" square strips of beech and are placed so that the center of the runner is precisely in the middle of the front drawer opening.

To mark out their precise length, set the case on its back, then take a scrap piece of ¾" material and put it on the inside face of the backboard. A piece of ¾" scrap is used because the drawer faces are ¾" thick, and this will ensure that the drawer stops with the front face of the drawer flush with the case sides. Put the runner in place on top of the scrap, then use a pencil to draw a line on the runner where it intersects with the front edge of the case. Cut the runner on this line using a fine crosscut backsaw.

The runners are screwed into place using countersunk ¾" #6 wood screws, one in each of the case side stiles and one into the center of each of the side panels.

The bottom drawer runners require a notch on each end to clear the bottom corner brackets.

Once the runners are affixed, rough-cut a piece of ¼" plywood to fit the case bottom. Screw it into place using ¾" wood screws. Once the bot-

**A finishing touch on the drawers.** With the drawers finished, bead the top and bottom edges of both drawers.

**Trim the plywood skin.** It should be flush with the frame pieces. Once the whole assembly is square, it's ready to be covered with molding.

**Scribe the top hinge before mortising.** Temporarily attach one side to the case, then use spacers to mark out the other half of the hinge.

tom is in place, plane the edges flush to the case using a sharp block plane.

## DRAWER CONSTRUCTION AND MOLDINGS

On the original, the drawers were simply butt-nailed together from plywood with an added front made from chestnut. I've chosen to replicate this in my chest (the original did survive a century of use), but you may choose to dovetail them together. To produce nailed-together drawers that approximate the original ones, I planed up stock to the proper width, which must accommodate the ¼" drawer bottoms, and then crosscut them to length. Nail them into a square drawer box and then nail on the ¼" plywood drawer bottoms.

Test fit them into the drawer openings and make any required adjustments to ensure they operate smoothly. The boxes should ideally stop about ¼" back from the front edge of the drawer runners.

Once the drawer boxes fit properly, it's time to make the faces. Dimension two pieces of beech to match the cut list. Shoot the ends so that they just slip into the opening, and then screw each face onto their respective drawer box. On the top drawer, the face should overhang the bottom of the box by ⅜" to engage the drawer runner/stop. On the bottom drawer, the opposite is true: the top edge of the drawer face should stick up that same ⅜" over the top of the drawer box. Fit the drawers at the same time to identify any clearance issues. Once any issues have been corrected with a sharp plane, cut a ⁵⁄₁₆" bead along the top and bottom edge of each drawer, four beads in all.

When that is done, the drawers are finished.

The final step on the case is to produce a run of molding to wrap around the case along the bottom. This helps to hide the plywood bottom and provides a finished look. The molded board should be slightly narrower, perhaps ⅛", than the bottom front rail. Miter the moldings and then attach them with wood screws from the inside. You may find it beneficial to temporarily remove the plywood case bottom when attaching the moldings. If you do so, make sure to use a scrap piece of plywood as a spacer to ensure that you overhang the moldings over the bottom case edge far enough to account for the thickness of the bottom.

### THE TILTING TOP

The top subframe is made from ¾" x 1¼" beech. Each corner is half-lapped and then held together with a single wood screw driven in from the top face (so that no screwheads are visible on the inside). I make the top so that it overhangs about ⅛" over the case front and sides while holding the back edge flush with the case back. This will make the top easy to open later on without significantly impacting the top's ability to protect the contents inside from dust and moisture. Begin by measuring the top of the case and then add ¼" to the width and ⅛" to the depth and cut the pieces to those newly revised lengths. Half-lap the corners by laying the front and back frame pieces on top of the two side pieces in a square frame, then marking the shoulders on the components. You'll be cutting away half the thickness

## CUT LIST & MATERIALS

| | NO. | ITEM | T | W | L | MATERIAL |
|---|---|---|---|---|---|---|
| ☐ | 2 | Side upper rails | ¾ | 2 | 9 | Chestnut |
| ☐ | 2 | Side bottom rails | ¾ | 4½ | 9 | Chestnut |
| ☐ | 4 | Side stiles | ¾ | 2 | 11¼ | Chestnut |
| ☐ | 2 | Side panels | ¼ | 6 | 10 | Plywood |
| ☐ | 1 | Front top | ¾ | 2⅞ | 21 | Chestnut |
| ☐ | 1 | Front bottom | ¾ | 2 | 21 | Chestnut |
| ☐ | 1 | Case back | ¾ | 11¼ | 22½ | Beech |
| ☐ | 1 | Case bottom | ¼ | 13 | 22½ | Plywood |
| ☐ | 1 | Top well bottom | ¼ | 11½ | 21 | Plywood |
| ☐ | 2 | Top well side strips | ½ | ½ | 10½ | Beech |
| ☐ | 2 | Top well front/back strips | ½ | ½ | 21 | Beech |
| ☐ | 2 | Lid subframe sides | ¾ | 1¼ | 13 | Chestnut |
| ☐ | 2 | Lid subframe front/back | ¾ | 1¼ | 22¾ | Chestnut |
| ☐ | 1 | Lid panel | ¼ | 13 | 22¾ | Plywood |
| ☐ | 1 | Lid interior facing top | ¼ | ~10½ | ~20¼ | Plywood |
| ☐ | 2 | Top drawer runners | ¾ | ¾ | 11½ | Beech* |
| ☐ | 2 | Bottom drawer runners | ¾ | 2 | 11½ | Beech |
| ☐ | 4 | Drawer sides | ¾ | 2½ | 11 | Chestnut |
| ☐ | 2 | Drawer backs | ¾ | 2½ | 21 | Chestnut |
| ☐ | 2 | Drawer fronts | ¾ | 2½ | 19½ | Chestnut |
| ☐ | 2 | Drawer bottoms | ¼ | 11¾ | 21 | Plywood |
| ☐ | 2 | Drawer faces | ¾ | 2¾ | 21 | Beech |
| ☐ | 2 | Case molding sides | ¾ | 2 | 13 | Beech |
| ☐ | 1 | Case molding front | ¾ | 2 | 24½ | Beech |
| ☐ | 1 | Top molding front | ¾ | 1¼ | 24½ | Beech |
| ☐ | 2 | Top molding sides | ¾ | 1¼ | 13 | Beech |
| ☐ | | Dowel joinery | ¼-dia. | | | Dowel |
| ☐ | 8 | Corner brackets | | | | Brass |
| ☐ | 1 | Continuous hinge | | | | Brass |
| ☐ | 1 | Chain | | | | |
| ☐ | 2 | Sash handles | | | | Brass |
| ☐ | 4 | Pull handles | | | | Brass |

* Centered to opening, screwed to side, and set ¾" from opening.

**EXPLODED DRAWERS**

**3D VIEW**

**SIDE VIEW**

**FRONT VIEW**

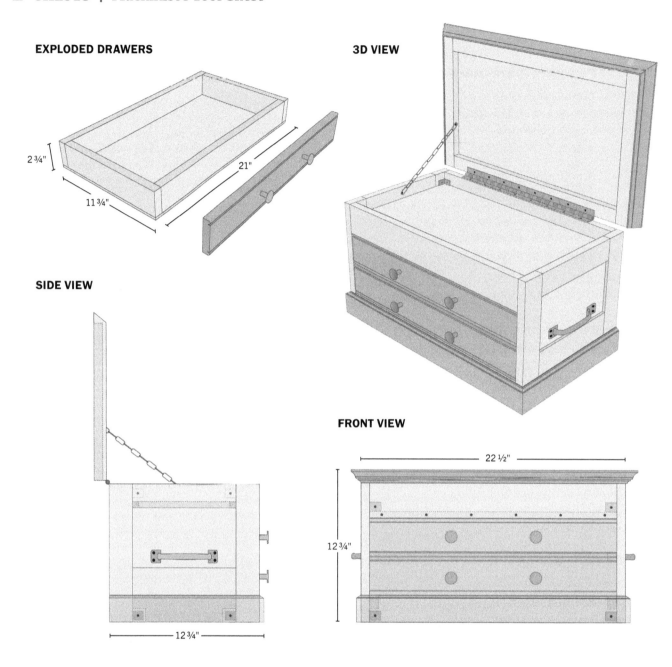

of each frame piece, so mark out ⅜" away from the bottom face on each using a marking gauge. Using a rip-filed backsaw, remove the bottom ⅜" on the front and back pieces and the top ⅜" on the two side pieces. Cut the shoulders with a crosscut-filed backsaw. Use a sharp chisel to refine the joint, then test-fit the frame.

Each corner should overlap properly, producing a flat frame that's square. Then, pilot-drill each corner and drive in a ¾" wood screw.

The frame is skinned on the top with a ¼" piece of plywood. Use whatever species you desire. (I happened to have a good-looking piece of red oak.) Cut it to rough size, and then

glue it down to the top of the frame using long beads of wood glue. Clamp it down then set it aside to dry. When it's dry, plane all four sides of the top skin flush to the frame using a sharp block plane. Install the top using a continuous hinge, mortising as necessary to ensure a flush, tight fit between the top and the lid.

When you've got the hinge installed correctly, remove the top from the hinge; cut and fit another piece of ¼" plywood to the inside of the frame so that it fits inside the center edge of the frame, and glue it down to the inside of the top skin. This provides a more attractive inside surface than whatever is on the back side of the top plywood skin.

Once the top is reinstalled, make a run of 1¼" tall, ¾" wide molding. The profile is up to you but I used a small ogee with a fillet. Wrap the molding with miters around the two sides and front edge of the top then glue and nail it in place with the top edge of the molding flush with the plywood top skin.

## FINISHING TOUCHES

Install the handles. I used brass sash handles from the hardware store but feel free to be as fancy or as simple as you like. The important consideration here is to ensure that the handle is at least partially screwed into the side drawer runner. This provides a much stronger substrate for the screws over just attaching them into the side panels. It's acceptable to have a few screws that just go into the panel but at least half of them truly need to enter the runner.

To install the drawer pulls, make small pencil marks on the top edge of the case approximately 5" in from the sides of the case. Next, take a square and draw a light pencil line to extend both pencil marks down across both of the drawer faces. Then, divide each drawer width in half and make a light horizontal line across the previously drawn vertical lines. That intersection marks the point where the pull

**Install brass sash handles.** They should align with the drawer runner so that the screws have plenty of wood to bite into.

knobs should be installed. Pilot-drill and test-fit the pulls to ensure they line up properly.

Remove the hardware before finishing. Erase any stray pencil lines then sand the entire project to #220 grit. I finished the chest with my favorite wood finish ("boat soup"), which is nothing more than equal parts pine tar, turpentine, and linseed oil. I wiped three coats on the exterior and, after it dried, applied a coat of paste wax. I also applied paste wax to the drawer runners to help the drawers operate smoothly.

Once the finish has dried, the fun part begins: filling the chest with your prized collection and figuring out the best way to fit everything inside. Enjoy! ∎

# DOVETAILED, CURLY MAPLE TOOL CHEST

Build a custom tool chest to fit exactly the tools you want.

BY LOGAN WITTMER

I have a confession. I like nice tools. There's something about boutique tool makers that I love. I'm guessing it's the combination of high-quality tools and the maker's backstory that speaks to me. Understandably, most of the time, the tools from these types of companies are pretty pricey. With that being said, I've been tossing a lot of my tools into a tool tote over the last few years as I travel to give demonstrations or teach classes. Every time they rattle and bang together, I cringe. So, that's what drove me to build myself a nicer toolbox that would keep my tools protected.

The style of this tool chest is based on one that I saw in a David Barron video years ago. Mine is a bit bigger, and once it's loaded with tools, it's decently heavy. However, it's still fairly easy to carry to and from demonstrations, and it keeps everything safe and organized.

## CUSTOMIZATION IS KEY

Now, this project is probably a little different in that I'm fully expecting if someone builds a chest of this style, it will be completely different than mine. And that's the point. I want to show you the process, but the sizing and customization is up to you, your tools, and what you want to store in your tool chest. To be honest, it doesn't even have to be a tool chest. It could be a hope chest, sewing chest, or anything else you could imagine.

From a sizing standpoint, the first thing I want to do is figure out exactly what tools will ride in it and divide them up into different groups. Of course, the heaviest items should always go in the bottom. As you can

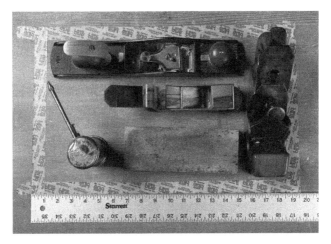

**Bottom of chest.** The heaviest tools live here. Just because the chest will hold these does not mean they will all make every journey with me.

**Tray.** The contents of the tray will shift as jobs or demonstrations change. To be honest, I know that it will probably be a catch-all, so the only organization that it will get will be a chisel tray to protect the edges.

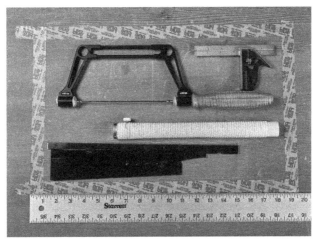

**Inside of lid.** Finally, this is the valuable real estate for some of the lighter, longer items. As needs evolve, I could see myself changing the tools and holders that are located inside the lid. Always keep your options open.

**Cut down to size.** A carcase saw makes quick work of breaking down rough stock into parts.

**Square up the stock.** A shooting board is an essential tool for squaring up boards and sizing parts in any hand tool shop.

**David Barron dovetail saw guide.** This is my go-to system for cutting dovetails.

**Continuing the dovetail cut.** After starting the kerf with the guide, I'll often pull the guide away and sneak down to the baseline.

see on page 75, that ends up being a low-angle jack plane, a smoothing plane, my miter plane, a few oil stones, and my oil can.

I suggest nesting your tools in a group and playing with the arrangement. It's important to see how they fit together. The layout I settled on can be seen on page 75. I used a few strips of painter's tape to rough in the box size. I had planned on my tool chest having a tray. Quite obviously, the tray will be about the same size as the box. Technically, it's a little smaller but close enough. Using the same painter's tape outline, I made sure that a vast majority of the tools I need were going to fit within the tray.

The third and final layer of my chest is the inside of the lid. This will contain the longer items that don't really fit in the tray once I include a chisel case there. My pull saw, coping saw, paring chisel, and square pretty much fill this out. Technically, I could probably squeeze a few more tools into the inside of the lid, but this is good for now.

**CASE CONSTRUCTION**

The carcase of the tool chest consists of the front, back, sides, and bottom. Here, I'll talk about building the carcase, but the lid and tray are pretty much identical, just a different size.

I start by breaking apart my stock into the necessary parts. For this chest, I chose some nicely figured soft maple. Something like pine or fir would work as well and be lighter, but I liked the look of this maple.

Because this is for my hand tools, I felt it would be bad ju-ju not to use as many hand tools in the construction

**The beginning.** Mark the lead edge of the workpiece on the router table fence.

**The end.** Mark the ending position of the workpiece on the fence.

**Start to rout.** Lower the workpiece onto the spinning bit and rout right to left.

**Complete the rout.** As you reach your stop mark, raise the workpiece off the bit.

as I could. A carcase saw rough cuts parts easily, and I used my shooting board and low-angle jack to make sure everything was square with equal lengths.

After sizing the parts, the majority of the work on the tool chest is cutting the dovetail joints. You could go with some fancy dovetails here if you want, but I chose tried-and-true through-dovetails. If you've never hand-cut dovetails, this is a great lit-tle project to try them out on. A step-by-step for cutting dovetails can be found on pages 76 to 78.

After cutting the joinery on all of the parts, you now have to rout a groove along the bottom edge of the inside of the box. This will be for the solid wood bottom. Routing this groove can be a little tricky, as you don't want to rout through the end of the tails—it would be visible on the finished box. Instead, I mark a line on

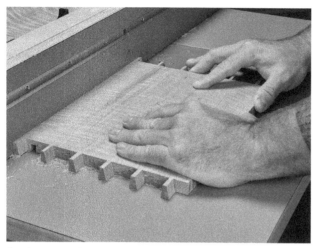

**Cut the groove.** The groove in the sides is positioned between the pins, and can be routed straight through.

**Rabbet.** Cut a rabbet around the top and bottom panel.

**Assemble the joints.** Start assembling the dovetail joints, then spread glue inside the tails and pins.

**Clamp.** Remember to apply even clamping pressure against the joints.

my router fence where I will plunge the front of the workpiece onto the bit (p. 77). Likewise, I mark a stopping point where I will stop the workpiece and shut off the router (p. 77). Then, it's a simple matter of lining up the workpiece with the starting mark and lowering the workpiece over the running router bit. As I reach the stopping mark, I shut off the router and raise the workpiece off the bit. The groove falls between the pins on the sides, so you can just rout straight through the workpiece (top left).

After gluing up a pair of panels, one for the top and one for the bottom of the chest, cut them to size. The top and bottom will get a rabbet cut along the four edges. This forms a tongue that will fit in the groove you just made inside the case. A rabbet plane can take care of this quickly, however, I already had a dado blade loaded up in my table saw, so I buried

**Flush trim.** After cutting the parts at the band saw, use a pattern bit to flush trim them to a hardboard template. Do both the outside (left) and the inside (right).

it in an auxiliary fence and cut the rabbet there (p. 78, top right). Any fine-tuning to get it to fit nicely into the groove in the case parts can be done with a rabbeting block plane.

## GLUE IT UP

With the parts in hand, you can now assemble the carcase. When it comes to an assembly like this, slow and easy seems to work better for me. This means using a glue with a long open time, like epoxy or hide glue. I spread glue on the inside of each tail and pin (p. 78), and get the front and sides assembled. Slip the bottom into place and drive the back home.

You can clamp the case together using specially made spacers to put pressure on each tail, but I'll usually just grab medium F-style clamps and put one across every other tail or so. If you've laid everything out accurately, the case should be pretty self squaring, but I always check and make any adjustments with a clamp strung corner-to-corner.

With the case drying, it's a good time to get working on the tray if you're including one. I made mine with some swooping handles on

them—making a template out of hardboard then using it to flush-trim the handles to size seems to work the best. Before dovetailing, I shot all the parts so they just slipped into the case, and then I cut the joinery. During the clamp-up, I fit it inside the carcase to make sure they were both equally square. After a little sanding, the tray slipped into the carcase,

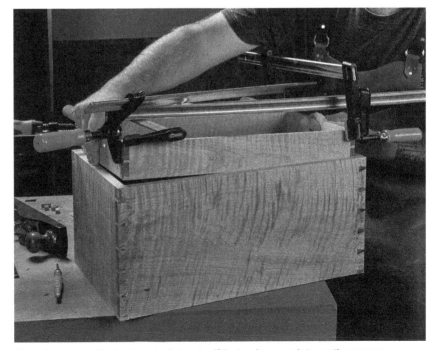

**Check for square.** The best way to determine if the tray is square is to use the carcase.

**FRONT VIEW**

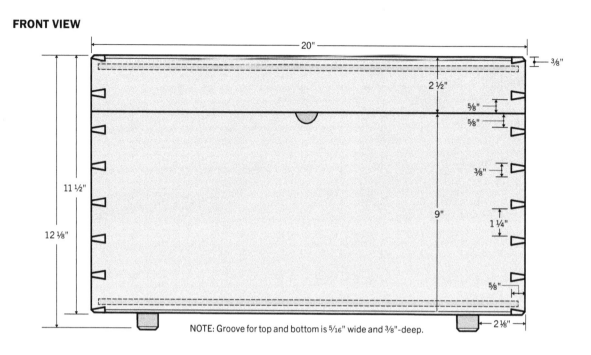

NOTE: Groove for top and bottom is ⁵⁄₁₆" wide and ³⁄₈"-deep.

**SIDE VIEW**

**EXPLODED VIEW**

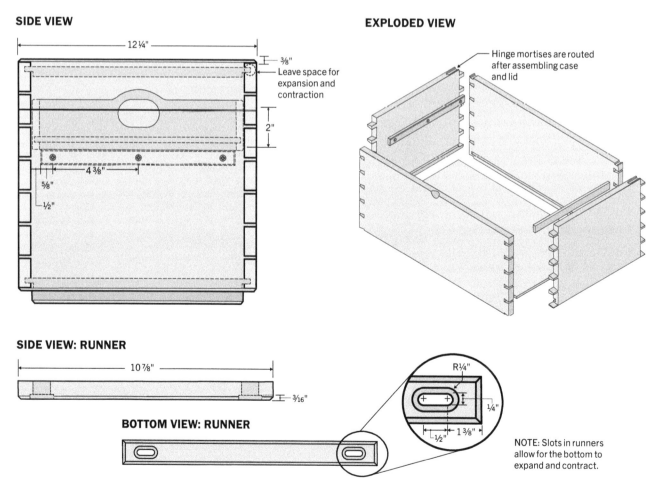

Leave space for expansion and contraction

Hinge mortises are routed after assembling case and lid

**SIDE VIEW: RUNNER**

**BOTTOM VIEW: RUNNER**

NOTE: Slots in runners allow for the bottom to expand and contract.

**EXPLODED VIEW: TRAY**

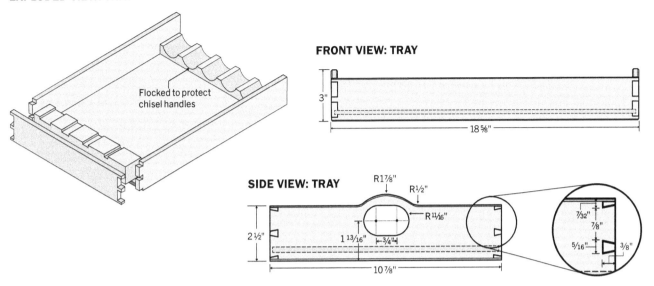

Flocked to protect chisel handles

**FRONT VIEW: TRAY**

3"

18 ⅝"

**SIDE VIEW: TRAY**

R1⅞"   R½"

R 11/16"

2 ½"

1 13/16"   ¾"

10 ⅞"

7/32"   ⅞"

5/16"   ⅜"

**TOP VIEW: CHISEL RACK HANDLE BLOCK**

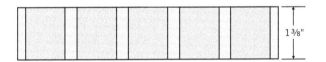

1 ⅜"

**TOP VIEW: CHISEL RACK BLADE BLOCK**

⅛"   ¼"   ⅜"   ½"   ¾"

15/16"

**SIDE VIEW: CHISEL RACK HANDLE BLOCK**

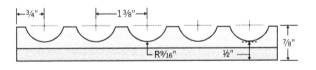

¾"   1 ⅜"

R9/16"   ½"

⅞"

**SIDE VIEW: CHISEL RACK BLADE BLOCK**

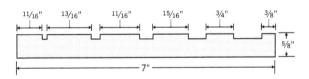

11/16"   13/16"   11/16"   15/16"   ¾"   ⅜"

7"

5/8"

**SIDE VIEW: CHISEL RACK**

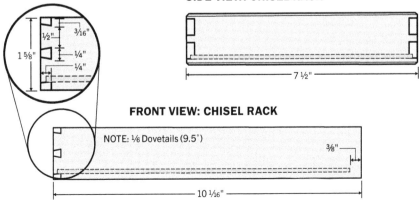

½"   3/16"

1 ⅝"   ¼"

¼"

7 ½"

**FRONT VIEW: CHISEL RACK**

NOTE: ⅙ Dovetails (9.5°)

⅜"

10 1/16"

## CUT LIST & MATERIALS

| | NO. | ITEM | DIMENSIONS | | |
|---|---|---|---|---|---|
| | | | T | W | L |
| **TOOL CHEST** | | | | | |
| ☐ | 2 | Front/back | 5/8 | 19 5/8 | 9 |
| ☐ | 2 | Sides | 5/8 | 12 1/4 | 9 |
| ☐ | 2 | Bottom/lid panel | 5/8 | 19 3/8 | 11 1/2 |
| ☐ | 2 | Runners | 3/4 | 10 7/8 | 1 |
| ☐ | 2 | Lid front/back | 5/8 | 19 3/8 | 2 1/2 |
| ☐ | 2 | Lid sides | 5/8 | 12 1/4 | 2 1/2 |
| ☐ | 2 | Tray cleats | 5/16 | 3/4 | 10 |
| **CHEST TRAY** | | | | | |
| ☐ | 2 | Front/back | 3/8 | 18 3/8 | 2 1/2 |
| ☐ | 2 | Sides | 3/8 | 3 | 10 7/8 |
| ☐ | 1 | Bottom | 1/4 | 18 1/8 | 10 5/8 |
| **CHISEL RACK** | | | | | |
| ☐ | 1 | Front | 1/4 | 7 1/2 | 1 5/8 |
| ☐ | 2 | Sides | 1/4 | 10 1/16 | 1 5/8 |
| ☐ | 1 | Bottom | 1/8 | 9 1/2 | 7 1/4 |
| ☐ | 1 | Handle block | 7/8 | 1 3/8 | 7 |
| ☐ | 1 | Blade block | 5/8 | 15/16 | 7 |
| **SUPPLIES** | | | | | |
| ☐ | | Flocking for chisel rack | | | |
| ☐ | 2 | Large brass jewelry box side rail hinges, such as Neat Elite | .17 | .37 | 2.36 |

All parts are curly maple except the tray and chisel rack bottoms, which are plywood.

slowly lowering on a small cushion of air. A perfect fit!

The lid to the box follows the same steps as the base. Once the lid is complete, I attached the two using some side rail hinges. The groove for the hinges can be routed easily at the router table. You could just as easily use butt hinges for the same effect. The final steps before adding tool storage are to add a pair of runners on the bottom to lift the chest off the bench, add some cleats to the inside for the tray to sit on, and to chamfer the top and bottom edges.

## CUSTOMIZATION

Now is where you can really tailor this tool chest to fit your needs. For mine, I divided the inside of the carcase with cleats. These keep my planes in place, and I even made a cleat for my router plane to sit on.

I know that my tray is going to be a catch-all, so the only storage I made on this was a small chisel case with inserts that cradle the chisels.

The lid was the trickiest storage of them all. Here, you'll need to get creative with your tool holders. Mine uses a combination of cleats, magnets, and toggles to lock everything in place. The biggest thing is to keep the perimeter of the lid clear, as the tray projects slightly into the lid.

As far as hardware items, I chose not to put handles on the side of my chest. Instead, I plan to pick it up from the bottom of the box. However, you could easily install handles on the side.

For the lid, it's easy to lift with the rabbet around the top, but I also added a small thumb notch to help lift it up. I cut this in with a carving gouge. A screw-on style handle would work as well.

When it comes to finishing the tool chest, you can take your pick. Paint, varnish, and polyurethane would all be great choices. For a figured wood like this, I start with a base of tinted shellac, followed by a light sanding. After cutting back the shellac, I apply a Danish oil over top, letting it soak in before buffing it off. Once the finish is dry, a quick coat of paste wax allows the tray to slip into place, and then it's ready to report for duty. ■

**A peek inside.** The finished box houses the tools that I use while demonstrating, but I could add extra tools or change out cleats as necessary.

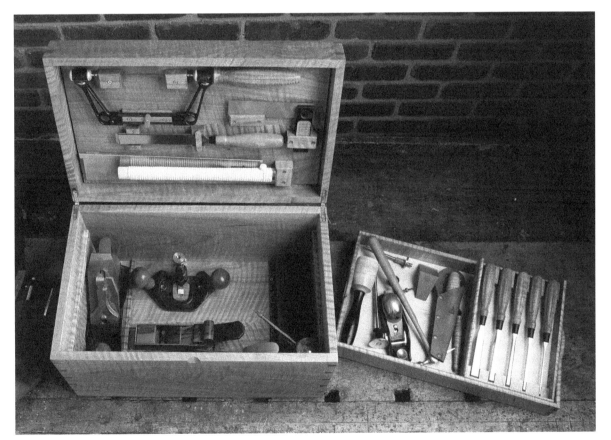

**Ample storage.** The inside of the case has cleats for the tray to sit on, as well as cleats screwed into the bottom to position planes. By using screws, the cleats can be removed and adapted as tools change.

# 10-DRAWER TOOL CHEST

## Store your smaller tools in style with a tool chest that's surprisingly simple to build.

BY JIM STACK

**M**ost woodworkers have dozens of tools that are small, such as screwdrivers, files, chisels, pliers, dividers, and compasses. All these can be stored in shallow drawers, which is where this chest comes into the picture. The design for the chest came from two inspirations. One was a Craftsman-style bookcase plan. The sides and top are shaped like the bookcase, and the chest is made of quartersawn white oak. The other inspiration came from multi-drawer chests that were made years ago to store sheet music. This chest was assembled with butt joints and screws. I countersunk the screws and plugged the holes with ⅜" redheart plugs. The drawer pulls also are redheart, which I cut using a ½" plug cutter. ■

**The first step.** Cut the sides ⅜" narrower than the finished dimension. Then cut the ¼" x ¼" dados for the drawers. Glue a ⅜" x ¾" strip to the back of each side. This strip covers where the dados exit the sides, creating a stopped dado.

**Draw the top arcs.** There is one on each side. Trammel points mounted on a stick are great for drawing arcs. A little trial and error is involved here unless you can figure the radius using math. I try connecting the dots, moving the pencil up or down the stick until I find the radius that works. If you don't have trammel points, drive a nail through a stick at one end. This is your fixed point. Use a small clamp or rubber band to hold a pencil anywhere you need along the length of the stick to draw your arc.

**Draw the bottom arcs.** Again, there is one on each side. When laying out the radii at the bottom of the sides, use a small, round object to draw the small radius that defines each foot.

**Join them.** Connect these two small radii with an arc that is 1" high from the bottom of the side.

**Drill.** Make holes with the same radius as the small arcs and connect them by cutting the larger arc with a jigsaw or band saw.

**Smooth and shape the arcs.** Use a rat-tail file or curved rasp.

## CUT LIST & MATERIALS

| | NO. | ITEM | DIMENSIONS (INCHES) | | | MATERIAL | COMMENTS |
|---|---|---|---|---|---|---|---|
| | | | T | W | L | | |
| ☐ | 2 | Sides | ¾ | 12* | 24 | White oak | Width includes ⅜" edging. |
| ☐ | 1 | Top | ¾ | 11¼ | 15 | White oak | |
| ☐ | 1 | Bottom | ¾ | 11¼* | 15 | Plywood | Width includes ⅜" edging. |
| ☐ | 1 | Back | ¾ | 15 | 23* | Ply/oak | Top crown is 2¼" wide, glued to ply. |
| ☐ | 10 | Drawer fronts | ½ | 1⅝ | 14¹⁵⁄₁₆ | White oak | |
| ☐ | 20 | Drawer sides | ½ | 1⅝ | 10¼ | Poplar | |
| ☐ | 10 | Drawer backs | ½ | 1⅝ | 14¹⁵⁄₁₆ | Poplar | |
| ☐ | 10 | Drawer bottoms | ¼ | 11¼ | 15½ | Plywood | Trim sides to fit after drawers are assembled. |
| ☐ | 10 | Drawer pulls | ½-dia. | | ½ | Redheart | Cut with ½" plug cutter. |
| ☐ | 22 | Plugs | ⅜-dia. | | ~¼ | Redheart | Cut with ⅜" plug cutter. |
| ☐ | 2 | Side strips | ⅜ | ¾ | 24 | White oak | Glued to back edge of sides. |
| ☐ | 1 | Bottom strip | ⅜ | ¾ | 15 | White oak | Glued to front edge of bottom. |
| ☐ | 1 | Back crown | ¾ | 2¼ | 15 | White oak | Glued to top edge of back. |
| ☐ | 10 | Dowel rods | ⅛-dia. | | ¾ | Hardwood | |

\* Measurement is finished dimension and includes solid-wood edging.

**Assemble and plug.** Glue the back crown on top of the plywood back panel. Make the arc on the crown as you did for the sides. Cut the top and bottom panels to size, then glue a ⅜" x ¾" strip on the front of the bottom panel. Assemble the chest using 2" screws. Cut the plugs and glue them in place to cover the screw heads.

**A close look at the arcs.** Here you can see how the two arcs meet nicely at the back corner of the case. These little details will make the sides and back flow together nicely.

**TOP VIEW**

Top

11¼"

½"d x ½" plug

16½"

**DRAWER ASSEMBLY**

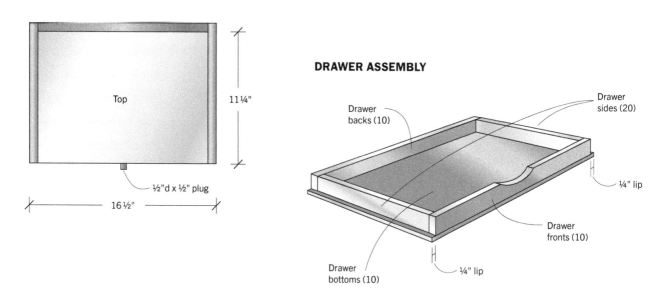

Drawer
backs (10)

Drawer
sides (20)

¼" lip

Drawer
fronts (10)

Drawer
bottoms (10)

¼" lip

**FRONT VIEW**

Back crown

1½"

⅝"

1⅞" typ.

Drawer
fronts (10)

Drawer
pulls (10)

Side

1"

15"

Bottom

**SIDE VIEW**

24"

Back

Plugs

1"

10"

1"

**Make the drawer frames.** Cut the parts to size. The sides are captured between the front and back parts, so glue-up can be done with two clamps. I just used glue on these butt joints. I know what you're thinking: Why would he use just glue and no fasteners or other joinery to strengthen this joint? Well, after the plywood bottoms are glued in place, the drawers are quite strong. (If you would like to use fasteners, please do so. Screws or dowels would work well.)

**Glue and clamp.** I use bench horses all the time to hold parts for gluing. Several drawers can be glued at one time. After applying glue to the bottoms, hold them in place with a few small brads or nails. Then stack up a few drawers and clamp them while the glue dries. This also helps keep the drawers flat.

**Rout a bead.** When the glue has dried on the drawers, rout the ¼" bead on the top and bottom of the drawer fronts. The drawer bottoms are the perfect thickness to accept the radius of the bead. (See below.)

**SIDE VIEW DETAIL: DRAWER**

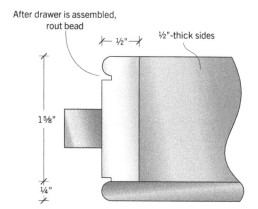

After drawer is assembled, rout bead

½"

½"-thick sides

1 ⅝"

¼"

**Make the pulls.** If necessary, fit the drawers by planing or sanding the sides of the bottoms that fit into the grooves to ensure the drawers slide smoothly. Then cut the plugs for the drawer pulls. I attached the pulls with an ⅛" dowel rod. Drill a hole in the center of the plug, and a matching hole in the drawer front. Glue the pulls in place, then sand and finish the chest and drawers.

# 12 RULES FOR TOOL CHESTS

## Don't reinvent the wheel when storing your tools; a proper chest is still the best.

BY CHRISTOPHER SCHWARZ

When I tell people that I've worked out of a traditional tool chest for 15 years, they look at me as if I'm someone who has not yet discovered the joys of indoor plumbing.

They say, "Haven't you tried a wall cabinet? Or built storage below your workbench? Why not a series of open shelves next to your bench?"

The truth is that I've tried all those methods, yet I still return to my tool chest. It holds every hand tool a woodworker could want. It protects the tools from dust (which contains salt and encourages rust). And I can get to every tool in the chest with only one hand motion.

In other words, it's tidy, protective, and efficient. What more could you want?

The objections that most woodworkers have to tool chests are generated by people who have never worked out of a chest or who have worked out of a modern chest.

You see, most new chests that I've encountered are all wrong. They are usually too small to be useful. Most of these mini-chests were built in woodworking classes and needed to be transported home easily—hence their squat stature.

**A box chock-full of tradition.** This tool chest, which was designed from time-tested examples, holds every hand tool you need, protects those tools from dust, and keeps everything just one hand motion away.

And the interiors of these modern chests are poorly divided. Either the woodworker has French-fitted every tool into a space, which is inflexible, or he or she has almost no way of dividing up the chest, so the tools are piled at the bottom.

For the last couple years I have studied many ancient chests. And what I found was surprising. Old chests are quite similar in size and in the way their interiors are divided. The other thing that is surprising is how plain most old chests are—inside and out.

Most of the tool chests we see in books are the fancy ones, on which some enterprising soul spent months adding veneer and inlay to the interior. These kinds of chests are rare in the wild. Old chests usually have three compartments in the bottom for planes and saws and three sliding trays above for the remaining tools. No inlay. No banding.

As I studied these old chests, I started developing 12 rules that describe their size and construction. While not all old chests follow all these rules, the best chests obey the majority of them.

### RULE NO. 1: AS LONG AS YOUR TOOL, PLUS SOME

The sizes of woodworking tool chests are fairly standard—between 35" and 43". This range allows the chest to hold full-size handsaws, which have a 26"-long blade, plus another 5" of wooden tote. Ripsaws can have an even longer blade, up to 30". Plus you need to get your hand in there to grab the tote of your longest saw. In addition to long saws, the chest needs to hold a jointer plane. While metal planes top out at about 24" long, wooden-bodied planes can be as much as 30" long.

Bigger isn't always better, however. A chest that is longer than 43" will make it hard to transport in a carriage or minivan.

So when you are sketching the length of your chest, measure your longest saw, add 5" so you can get your hand in there easily, and add a

**The long of it.** My 24"-long jointer plane is the biggest plane I own. So I made sure that it would fit in the bottom of my chest and could be easily removed.

**Put your right hand in.** Secure your body against the rim of the chest with your off-hand. Root around for the tool you need with your dominant hand. No deep-knee bends are necessary.

couple inches for the thickness of the material. That will easily get you to 37" to 40" if you use full-size saws.

## RULE NO. 2: TALL ENOUGH TO MAKE A HUMAN TRIPOD

Short tool chests are difficult to use. They are about 14" to 16" high, and when you put them on the floor, it is painful to bend over to fetch a tool. So you put them on top of your workbench or table saw. Now the toolbox is taking up valuable space.

Traditional toolboxes are usually about 22" to 27" high. Those heights are ideal for the human form. The rim of the tool chest is below the pivot point of your waist. So you bend over and place your off-hand on the rim of the chest to stabilize yourself as you use your dominant hand to shift trays around. Your off-hand becomes the third leg of a human tripod.

Naturally, the extra height gives you more room for tool trays, saw tills or chisel racks. It also makes the chest a nice height for sitting while working at the bench.

## RULE NO. 3: A DEPTH TO MATCH YOUR REACH

The depth of the chest is usually about the same dimension as its height. This makes sense for a lot of reasons. For one, it looks nice. A square profile is a pleasing form. But it also makes practical sense. A shallow tool chest wouldn't be as stable, especially with its lid open. A deeper chest would be a pain to use. Imagine a 36"-deep chest. Your arms would have a heck of a time fetching tools in the back.

So now we have sketched out a shell that's about 38" long, 24" high,

and 24" deep, maybe a little smaller or a little bigger depending on the material on hand. Speaking of material, what wood should we use for the chest? The natural inclination is to use something strong, such as oak or maple. But tool chests in these materials aren't common.

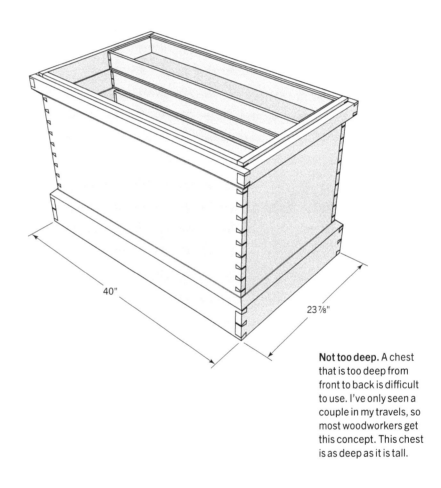

40"

23 7⁄8"

**Not too deep.** A chest that is too deep from front to back is difficult to use. I've only seen a couple in my travels, so most woodworkers get this concept. This chest is as deep as it is tall.

### RULE NO. 4: REDUCE THE WEIGHT; INCREASE THE JOINERY

One of the guiding principles of chest construction is to make the chest both lightweight, to make it easier to move, and strong, because the chest might take a beating on a voyage.

Lightweight woods aren't typically as strong as heavy woods. So here's what you do: Use a lightweight wood such as pine. But join the corners using a bombproof joint: through-dovetails. Use this approach for every component of the chest, except for the parts that endure friction. Soft and lightweight woods are easily worn away if they rub constantly against other parts.

**Light but strong.** If you use pine for your shell (and you should), then you should beef up the thickness a bit. I like 7⁄8"—some people go for the full inch.

The best strategy is to use oak in certain areas of the chest. That means oak drawer runners and oak drawer bottoms—if your drawer bottoms rest on your runners. If, instead, your drawer bottoms are captured inside your tool trays, then make the side pieces out of oak. Use pine for the rest of the parts and dovetail every corner.

### RULE NO. 5: MAKE A THICK SHELL

Let's talk about the four walls of the chest. That's where material selection and construction begins. Old woodworking books are specific about the material for the shell: the clearest pine possible, free of knots and sapwood.

This might seem odd considering that the chest will be painted, but it's good advice. One of the antique chests I owned had several knots on the back. When I bought it, a couple of the knots had fallen out, and after moving the chest to the Midwest, a couple more fell out. Those I glued back in with epoxy. Why be so fussy about knots? They expose your tools to dust, which carries salts, which will corrode your tools.

Most tool chests have shells made from pine that is between 7⁄8" and 1" thick. Early furniture was more likely to have thicker structural components, so a 3⁄4"-thick shell would be unusual.

So why not make the shell out of 1½" material? You could, but dovetailing those corners would be a major pain because your material is so thick—you'd probably have to use a tenon saw to cut the dovetails. And I don't think the extra-thick material would add meaningful strength.

Chests made from ⅞" material stand up just fine for a couple hundred years.

### RULE NO. 6: THE BOTTOM SHOULD BE NAILED. BUT WHY?

So after all this talk about dovetails, it might seem odd that I recommend tonguing and grooving the chest's bottom boards and nailing them on. Why not put in a solid bottom that's captured in a groove?

A single solid-panel bottom will move a lot compared to five or six individual bottom boards, which will share the seasonal expansion and contraction. So if you use a solid-panel bottom, you must leave a sizable gap for the panel to swell and shrink in the groove in the shell, which isn't ideal. You want everything to be as tight as possible.

There are other good reasons to use individual boards secured by nails. If the bottom gets damaged, replacing one cracked board is easier than replacing an entire panel, no matter how the bottom is attached. And replacing one nailed-on board is easier than replacing a board secured in a groove.

The bottom of the chest is the most susceptible to damage, but not the kind of damage that some extra thickness will fix. The bottom boards are prone to rot, especially in a leaky basement shop.

### RULE NO. 7: SKIRT, DUST SEAL, AND MITERS

The chest's skirt and dust seal are nearly as prone to damage as the chest's bottom. They are the first line of defense when the chest is slid onto a truck or rammed by machinery.

**Fixable.** By securing the bottom with nails instead of a fancier joint, you are making the chest easier to repair in the future. Bottom boards can rot.

**Not mitered.** Dovetail your skirt and dust seal to the shell to ensure they stick around. Literally.

The skirt and dust seal (the skirt near the top rim of the shell) should be bulletproof. Simple miters will not do.

Dovetail the corners of your skirt and dust seal. Yes, it's a pain to fit everything around the shell. But a dovetailed skirt and seal will last forever. Their corners will never open. So the exterior of your chest will look as sturdy in 100 years as the day you built it.

### RULE NO. 8: DON'T BLOW IT ON THE LID

There are several ways to make a lid. Some work great. Some are temporary.

Some chests feature a single flat panel of wood trimmed on three edges with narrow stock that interlocks with the dust seal attached to the shell. These lids shrink, crack, and break loose from their trim. Time is unkind to these chests.

**Better lid.** A frame-and-panel lid with a raised panel is about as robust as you can get without adding lots of weight.

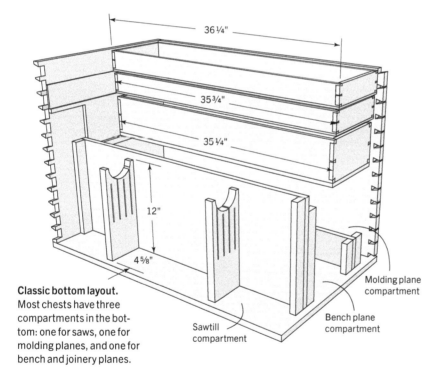

**Classic bottom layout.** Most chests have three compartments in the bottom: one for saws, one for molding planes, and one for bench and joinery planes.

Sawtill compartment

Bench plane compartment

Molding plane compartment

36 ¼"

35 ¾"

35 ¼"

12"

4 ⅝"

Duncan Phyfe (1768–1854), one of the most celebrated 19th-century cabinetmakers, used a flat panel with breadboard ends for the lid of his chest. This lid has survived fairly well, though there is still going to be movement that can interfere with your lock hardware.

The best solution is to build the lid as a frame-and-panel assembly. This confines almost all of the wood movement to the panel, which floats harmlessly in the middle of the rails and stiles.

So you could build the lid like a raised-panel door—except for the panel part. You want the panel to be stout because it will take a beating. So the joint between the panel and the door frame is critical. You don't really want to thin down the edges of the panel like you would when making a door panel. Thin edges will weaken the panel.

The old-school solution here is to plow a groove in the four edges of the panel so the panel will interlock with the rails and stiles. This keeps the joint between the panel and frame as stout as possible and the panel will be raised above the frame of the lid.

There is no downside to this approach. There are no weak spots on the lid. There is no significant wood movement along the edges or ends of the lid; the trim around it will stay put. It is a permanent lid.

### RULE NO. 9: DIVIDE THE BOTTOM LAYER

With the exterior shell designed, we can now move to divvying up the inside of the chest. I am struck by how consistently early chests are laid out. And after trying out several arrangements, I've concluded that the old ways are good.

American tool chests tend to have two things on the bottom layer of the tool chest: planes (bench, molding, and joinery planes) and saws. Some English chests put the saws in a till affixed to the underside of the chest's lid, some did not. Some American chests would put a saw or two on the lid at times, but mostly the saws went in a rack near the front of the chest.

The back of the chest is a good place for molding planes and rabbet planes. Set them on their toes with the wedges facing the inside of the chest. A dividing wall under the wedges will hold the planes upright. The good thing is that most molding planes are the same length and width. (Older planes are a little different, but those are fairly rare.) Storing the planes upright in your chest is ideal. This allows you to see their profiles and sizes.

This part of the chest will take up only a small part of the bottom area—about 3 ½" of space plus the thickness of the wall. There is lots of space left.

If you put the molding planes at the back, I recommend you put the saw till up at the front of the chest. The size of the saw till depends on how many large saws you own. Because I have only four long saws, my rack is only 4 ⅝" wide plus the width of the wall separating the rack from the rest of the chest.

The till is simple—a couple boards with kerfs sliced in them to hold the sawblades. Planning the tills is more difficult than making them. You want to consider the thickness of the totes and the size of the sawblades, both the length and the depth. And

## 'MORE VALUABLE THAN A SHIPLOAD OF GOLD'

Without a proper tool chest, the novel *The Life and Strange Surprizing Adventures of Robinson Crusoe* by Daniel Defoe would have been a whole lot shorter.

After Crusoe was shipwrecked off the coast of the Americas in the 1719 novel, he returned to the wrecked vessel to pillage it for supplies. Food, of course, was important to Crusoe. Second on the list: tools.

"And it was after long searching that I found out the carpenter's chest, which was, indeed, a very useful prize to me, and much more valuable than a shipload of gold would have been at that time. I got it down to my raft, whole as it was, without losing time to look into it, for I knew in general what it contained."

With the tools in the chest, Crusoe is able to build a whole life for himself, including a house and many niceties. Of course, first he has to learn to become a woodworker. And first he has to learn to sharpen.

On his second trip back to ship: "… I found two or three bags full of nails and spikes, a great screw-jack, a dozen or two of hatchets, and, above all, that most useful thing called a grindstone."

Crusoe's first project? Learning to process rough stock into boards so he could build a table and chair. His own words should be encouraging to beginning woodworkers who are teaching themselves the craft.

"And here I must needs observe, that as reason is the substance and origin of the mathematics, so by stating and squaring everything by reason, and by making the most rational judgment of things, every man may be, in time, master of every mechanic art. I had never handled a tool in my life; and yet, in time, by labour, application, and contrivance, I found at last that I wanted nothing but I could have made it, especially if I had had tools."

you want the till to hold your saws in a place where you can reach them without stooping too far over.

The rest of the space on the floor of the tool chest is reserved for bench planes and joinery planes. In my chest, I ended up with a space that measured more than 10" x 37". That is a lot of acreage. You should be able to fit all of the standard planes in there, plus have room for a few other things. Some woodworkers would fold their shop apron and use it to cover the bench planes.

Having the bench planes, saws, and molding planes at the bottom of the chest works well. For one thing, these tools have more mass than the

**Three trays.** Here you can see my three sliding trays arrayed so I can see everything in them. I'm only one hand motion away from accessing any of the three bins in the bottom of the chest.

smaller tools above, so this puts a lot of the weight at the bottom of the chest, lowering the center of gravity.

Also, when you work, the first task of the day is to remove the bench planes and put them under or on your bench. Then you remove the saws and hang them on the wall in front of you. So now there is a large part of the chest that you don't have to access. The molding planes can go on the bench—some woodworkers store them in a rack on their bench. But for most woodworkers, creating moldings makes up but a small part of the time on a project. So those planes stay safely down at the bottom of the chest until needed.

### RULE NO. 10: TRAYS
The simplest and best way to divide the upper section is to build trays

that slide forward and back. Two or three trays are typical. Chests that have trays that slide left and right are out there, though they are rare. Why? Probably because it makes it difficult to fetch the long tools below.

The trays slide forward and back on runners that are nailed and glued to the sides of the chest. These runners are like shallow steps up the side of the chest so that each tray can be pulled out of the chest should you need to repair it.

The joinery for your trays should be permanent. You want to minimize their weight and maximize their durability. I recommend using ½"-thick pine and dovetailing the corners. The bottoms should be thin slips of white oak that are nailed to the underside of the dovetailed trays. This makes the part that wears—the bottom—quite durable. By nailing the bottoms to the trays, I save a little space compared to grooving the bottoms in, and I make it easier to repair the bottoms if they are ever wrecked.

I had room for three trays in my latest chest: one that is 4¾" deep and two that are 2½" deep. You need only one deep tray. Shallow trays are better in almost all cases.

What goes in these trays, specifically? There are lots of ways to go. The point is to keep your arrangement flexible. Sometimes you will be doing a lot of boring. Other times a lot of hammering. The fewer dividers you add, the more flexibility you'll have in the long run.

### RULE NO. 11: STICKING STUFF TO THE LID AND WALLS
Don't forget that the front wall and the lid are good places to store flat

stuff. On the lid, some people put a framing square or a few squares. I've seen a few handsaws and backsaws hanging on the lid, too. On the front wall of the tool chest, you can hang try squares and joinery saws—this is the traditional approach. I simply rest my dovetail and carcase saws against the wall. Other chests have a rack on the front wall of the chest for chisels, augers, and other long and narrow tools—gimlets, awls, striking knives, gouges, and the like.

### RULE NO. 12: PAINT THE OUTSIDE

This is the easy part. The outside of a tool chest should be painted. The modern choice is to use milk paint, which is durable and looks better as it ages. We don't have lead-based paints available, which were the paints of choice in the pre-Industrial world.

Paint will keep your chest looking good for a long time. Anytime it gets beat up, you can renew the look with another coat of paint. A stain or clear finish cannot be renewed as easily. Plus, paint is the most weather-, UV- and abuse-resistant finish available.

On the inside of the chest, I recommend skipping a finish. If you must finish the inside, use shellac, which will cure quickly and won't leave a nasty oily smell like linseed oil will.

### DON'T BE A MODERN FAILURE

Many modern efforts to improve our workshops have been unsuccessful. We tried to re-engineer our workbenches so they were portable, and they became too lightweight and spindly. We redesigned the sawbench into plastic sawhorses that are the wrong height and are flimsy. We invented iron quick-release vises,

which won't hold much of anything relating to woodworking.

And we have done the same thing with tool chests.

Our woodworking ancestors may have been uneducated and illiterate, but they certainly weren't stupid. They had to make a living out of their tool chests, so the design and function of their tool storage was well-considered.

I also have found that a traditional tool chest has other lessons to teach—if you pay attention—including the fact that it holds just the right number of tools to build any piece of furniture—and no more tools than you actually need. ■

**It's clear.** A painted finish is the clear choice for a tool chest. The paint protects the chest from the harsh indignities of workshop life.

# TOMMY MAC'S TOOLBOX

## Combine power and hand tools to improve your joinery skills.

BY THOMAS J. MACDONALD

Building a toolbox much like this one was a real turning point in my woodworking career. It was 1999 and I had begun classes at Boston's North Bennet Street School's Cabinet and Furniture Making program. At the time, I was a pretty good carpenter and could build plywood cabinets using power tools, but I was pretty inexperienced when it came to crafting fine furniture. Designing and building a toolbox was one of our first project assignments at school.

The experience was, for me, way more than a project; it was my introduction to hand tools and more advanced joinery. Years later, I realize just how much this project influenced my woodworking. While building it, I was learning the harmony of using both power and hand tools.

Now, it's one of my favorite projects—and it's featured in season three of my PBS television show, *Rough Cut—Woodworking with Tommy Mac.*

If you're new to woodworking, or haven't learned basic hand-tool skills, this project could have a similar influence on you. Don't worry about the joints being a perfect fit. It's a shop project, after all.

## MILL YOUR LUMBER IN STAGES

I prepare stock in a couple sessions at least a day apart. This is meant to minimize wood movement while also allowing for it. As a rule of thumb, avoid taking more than ¼" of wood off the thickness of a board in one milling. I call the first session "rough mill" because I cut the parts out of the rough board, leaving about 1" over in length, ½" over in width, and ⅛" over in thickness.

First, flatten one face on the jointer. Check the grain direction of the wood and watch for tear out. Take off about ¹⁄₁₆" with each pass until the face is flat. Next, straighten one edge with the jointed face against the fence. Make sure the fence is 90° to the bed of the jointer.

When the jointer work is done, move to the planer and make the opposite face parallel (to avoid tear out, whichever end trailed over the jointer should lead over the planer). Run each part through the planer with the jointed face down. Mill the

**Spring joint.** A slight concave shape planed onto mating surfaces of an edge joint allows you to clamp up with a single clamp across the center of the panel glue-up. Aim for a center that's recessed about ¹⁄₆₄".

boards to the sizes in the cutlist plus the overage just described.

Stack the parts with stickers between and align them vertically so each board is supported by the one below it. Leave the boards overnight, then repeat the milling process to bring the boards to final dimensions. Note that some parts must be fitted to the box rather than cut to dimensions now. After the second milling, remove any mill marks by skimming all surfaces with a handplane. Take light cuts to avoid changing the thickness or taking it out of square.

## SPRING JOINTS FOR GLUE-UPS

The wider outside case parts should be glued up from narrower boards; a full-width board may cup over time. Before edge-gluing, clamp each mating pair of boards face to face

**Pin spacing.** To get dovetail pins spaced equally, walk the compass across the work and make adjustments until the spacing is just right.

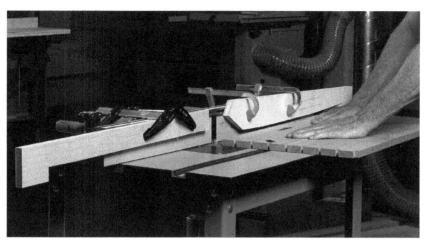

**Stop that rabbet.** Set up stop blocks on your router table's fence to register the front and back as you mill the rabbets in the back inside edges of the case sides.

and handplane the edges to "spring" the joint. Take a short pass along the middle of the edges, then another along more of the length and a final pass along the full length. The boards' jointed edges should touch at both ends with a tiny gap in the middle, about 1/64".

Glue up the boards starting with a single clamp in the middle. Add more clamps if necessary. After the glue has dried, clean up any excess and trim the parts to final width and length.

## THROUGH-DOVETAILS

Start by laying out the pins on the ends of the case side boards. Set a marking gauge to the thickness of the case parts and mark around the faces and edges at both ends of each board. Lay out the pins on the ends of a side board. Start by measuring and marking 3/16" from each edge. Then use a compass or dividers to make seven equal divisions between the 3/16" marks you just made (above). Start on one line and walk the dividers along to the other line. When they land directly on the line, the space is evenly divided. The points where the dividers hit are the center points of the pins. Transfer the divider marks to the outside face. Measure 3/16" on either side of the marks and, from that point, draw the dovetail angle across the end grain to the inside face. Square the lines down the inside and outside faces to the marking gauge line.

Now you can cut the pins. Carefully saw on the waste side of each pencil line, then use a coping saw to cut out the bulk of the waste. Use a chisel to chop to the marking gauge line. Chop halfway in, then flip the board and come in from the opposite face to finish the waste removal. Check the surfaces with a square and pare each cheek and shoulder until they are true.

When the pins are finished, scribe the tails. Stand each end of the pin board on its corresponding tail board. Align the inside face of the pins with the marking gauge line on the inside face of the top or bottom board. Trace the pins using a sharp pencil.

Square the tail lines across the ends of the boards, then cut carefully on the waste side of all of the lines. Saw out the bulk of the waste and chop to the marking gauge lines. Lightly test-fit each corner and mark where the joints are too tight to close. Use a chisel to pare the tails to fit. Do not adjust the pins.

## DADOS AND RABBETS

First, lay out the dados for the case dividers on the inside faces of the sides. The top one starts 2 3/8" from the top edge; the second dado is 4 7/8" from the top; the third is 8 1/4" from the top.

The dados are all ½" wide x ⅛" deep and are cut across the entire face.

To cut the dados, mount a ½" dado stack on the table saw to cut ⅛" deep. Make sure to cut the dados on the inside faces. Run the top edge of each side against the fence on all of the cuts. Once all of the dados are cut, use a router plane to clean up the dado bottoms.

Now, lay out and cut the ⅜" x ⅜" rabbets on the back inside corner of the case sides, top and bottom. The rabbets in the top and bottom run the full length of the edge. The rabbets on the sides stop ⅜" from each end.

Cut the rabbets at the router table. Set a straight bit to cut ⅜" from the tabletop and the fence. Run both the top and bottom all the way through. Set up to make the stopped cuts. With the router off, mark the front and back edges of the bit on the fence. Clamp front and back stops on the fence so that the bit will not cut past either end of the layout lines.

To make the cuts, set the back corner of the side against the rear stop and slowly move the piece toward the fence and into the cutter. Once it is against the fence, push the piece to the front stop, then slowly swing the back of the piece away from the cutter.

## GLUE UP THE CASE

Notch your clamping cauls around the pins so they press only on the tails. Glue and clamp the bottom corners first. Once the glue starts to set, remove the clamps and glue the top corners, checking for square. Now leave the clamps on until the glue has fully cured.

## MAKE THE CASE DIVIDERS

Frames divide the case and act as drawer supports. The outside corners of the frames are joined with bridle or slip joints. The two upper dividers have a middle rail with stub tenons.

Begin by cutting the slots in the long stiles. The slots are ¼" thick x 1¾" long, and go through the full width of the front and back frame parts, centered in the thickness of the parts. Put a ¼"-thick dado stack on your table saw set to cut 1¾" high. Cut the slots with the parts on end using a backer board, such as tenon-

ing jig, to support the piece. When done, cut grooves for the stub tenons in the front and back pieces. Without moving the fence, lower the dado stack to ¼" and cut grooves on the inside edges of the top two frames.

Now cut and fit the frame tenons using your dado stack and table saw. Run the stock flat on the saw table guided with the miter gauge. The dado stack should be set to cut just ⅛" high. Cut the top face of the tenons first, then fit the joint by trimming the bottom face. For the top two center rails, cut the tenons at the same time as the rest. After all of the joints are fit, trim the tenons on the center runners to ¼" long.

With the frame joinery complete, glue up the frames and fit them to the case. Make sure the frames are square. If necessary, clamp the slip joints closed so the joints don't flare out. Once the glue dries, flush the top surfaces at the joints with a handplane. Fit the frames to the dados in the case sides by planing the bottom surfaces.

When the frames are done, glue on the cherry divider faces. Mill them

**Ready, set, assemble.** When all the case joinery is completed, including dovetails, dados, and rabbets, the toolbox is ready for glue-up.

**Custom caul.** To make sure the dovetail joints seat completely, make a clamping caul that applies pressure on only the tails.

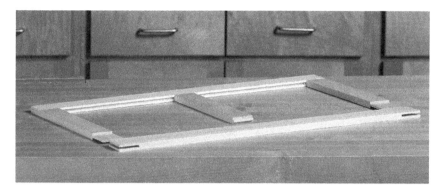

**Frame-up (top).** The case is divided using frames with slip joints at the ends and stub tenons where needed for a center divider. These frames support the drawers and fit in dados.

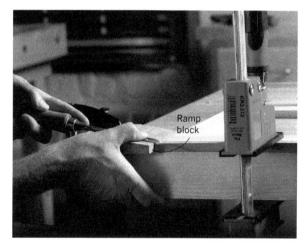

Ramp block

**Guided chisel (right).** As an aid to cutting the dovetails on the divider fronts, use a shop-made ramp block to guide the chisel and help achieve consistent sizes and angles.

the edge, mark ½" from one face. Tilt the table saw blade to 10° and set the fence just over ⅝" from the bottom of the blade. With the scrap on edge, rip the angle into the piece. Skim off any saw marks with a handplane.

Clamp the ramp block and divider as shown at center. The block should be perpendicular to the face piece and tight against its end. Chop down on the dado mark and remove chips until the chisel rides flat on the ramp block. Repeat this on the top and bottom of both ends of all of the dividers.

When done, fit the dividers to the case. Slide each divider in place then use a sharp pencil to trace the dovetails onto the front edges of the case. Remove the dividers, square the lines down the inside face, and mark the ¾" depth of the sockets. Saw, chop, and pare the sockets until the dividers fit snugly.

## PARTITION AND GUIDES

Mark the length of the dovetails and dados on the case top and second frame. The tails are ⁵⁄₁₆" from the inside edges of the top and frame. The dados are ⅛" deep x ½" wide, and centered in the case. Use a square, knife, and chisel to clear out the ¾"-long dados. Make sure the partition fits tightly in the dados. If not, either widen the dados or handplane the partition to fit. Once the partition fits, clamp the top divider to the second with the shoulders aligned on the ends, and scribe the dado across the face of the top divider. Cut the ½"-deep x ¾"-wide notch in the top divider and fit it to the partition.

Now cut the partitions to length. First, dry fit the frames in the case and measure the length of the par-

just thicker than the frames (divider fronts). Glue on the faces, allowing additional length on each end for the dovetails. Once the glue dries, handplane them flush to the frames. Lay out the length of the dovetails on the case sides. Slide each frame into place and mark the dovetail length and the bottom of the dovetail dado on the face piece. When done, cut each end of the cherry faces to length.

## DRAWER DIVIDER FRONT

I use a ramp block that helps me make the dovetails for the drawer divider front. To make it, mill a piece of scrap to ¾" thick x 4" wide (and make sure it's a scrap that allows you to work a safe distance from the blade). On

## CUT LIST & MATERIALS

| | NO | ITEM | DIMENSIONS (INCHES) | | | MATERIAL | COMMENTS |
|---|---|---|---|---|---|---|---|
| | | | T | W | L | | |
| ☐ | 2 | Top/bottom | 5/8 | 14 1/2 | 28 | Cherry | |
| ☐ | 2 | Sides | 5/8 | 14 1/2 | 13 1/4 | Cherry | |
| ☐ | 3 | Divider fronts | 1/2 | 1 3/4 | 27 | Cherry | |
| ☐ | 3 | Divider backs | 1/2 | 1 3/4 | 27 | Secondary | |
| ☐ | 6 | Divider sides | 1/2 | 1 3/4 | 13 3/8 | Secondary | |
| ☐ | 2 | Center runners | 1/2 | 1 3/4 | 13 3/8 | Secondary | Trim to fit. |
| ☐ | 3 | Divider faces | 1/2 | 3/4 | 27 5/8 | Cherry | Leave long. |
| ☐ | 1 | Vertical partition | 1/2 | 3/4 | 5 | Cherry | Leave long. |
| ☐ | 2 | Center drawer guides | 1/2 | 1/2 | 13 | Secondary | |
| ☐ | 4 | Back boards | 3/8 | 4 | 27 1/2 | Secondary | Shiplapped. |
| ☐ | 2 | Upper drawer fronts | 3/4 | 1 3/4 | 13 1/8 | Cherry | |
| ☐ | 4 | Upper drawer sides | 3/8 | 1 3/4 | 13 1/2 | Secondary | |
| ☐ | 2 | Upper drawer backs | 3/8 | 1 1/4 | 13 1/8 | Secondary | |
| ☐ | 2 | Narrow middle drawer fronts | 3/4 | 2 | 13 1/8 | Cherry | |
| ☐ | 4 | Narrow middle drawer sides | 3/8 | 2 | 13 1/2 | Secondary | |
| ☐ | 2 | Narrow middle drawer backs | 3/8 | 1 1/2 | 13 1/8 | Secondary | |
| ☐ | 1 | Wide middle drawer front | 3/4 | 2 7/8 | 26 3/4 | Cherry | |
| ☐ | 2 | Wide middle drawer sides | 3/8 | 2 7/8 | 13 1/2 | Secondary | |
| ☐ | 1 | Wide middle drawer back | 3/8 | 2 3/8 | 26 3/4 | Secondary | |
| ☐ | 1 | Lower drawer front | 3/4 | 3 7/8 | 26 3/4 | Cherry | |
| ☐ | 2 | Lower drawer sides | 3/8 | 3 7/8 | 13 1/2 | Secondary | |
| ☐ | 1 | Lower drawer back | 3/8 | 3 3/8 | 26 3/4 | Secondary | |
| ☐ | 4 | Narrow drawer bottoms | 3/8 | 14 5/8 | 12 3/4 | Secondary | Leave long. |
| ☐ | 2 | Wide drawer bottoms | 3/8 | 14 5/8 | 26 3/8 | Secondary | Leave long. |
| ☐ | 12 | Drawer stops | 1/8 | 1/2 | 5/8 | Secondary | |
| ☐ | 4 | Top drawer pulls | 3/4-dia. | | | Iron | |
| ☐ | 4 | Bottom drawer pulls | 1 1/8 | | | Iron | |

tition. Dovetail the ends using the ramp block that you used for the dividers. Mark the 1/4" dovetail length on the ends of the partitions. Set in the shoulders on the back and remove about 1/8" of the back of the tails. Use these notches to test the partition in the dados. Once the shoulders fit, cut the tails with the ramp block as before.

Fit the partition to the case. With the dividers in place, slide the partition into the dados and scribe the tails on the case and second divider. Mark the 5/8" depth of the tails as well. Remove the partition and divider to cut and fit the sockets. When done, glue in the dividers and partition. Start by sliding the dividers in almost completely, then apply glue to the

**Dovetail socket.** The socket for the case dovetail is located at the end of a shallow dado that houses the drawer divider.

**Upper drawers divided.** A vertical partition divides the case for the four narrower upper drawers. It is dovetailed like the divider fronts at the ends, and it is let into the middle of the top drawer divider with a simple notch.

front 2" and the dovetail. With the dividers in place, glue in the partition. Glue the center drawer runners on the top two dividers directly behind the partition. Use a square to make sure they are flush to the width of the partition and square to the front of the case.

### MAKE THE DRAWERS

On the inside face of each drawer part (except the bottoms), cut a ¼"-wide x ³⁄₁₆"-deep groove ¼" up from the bottom edge. Once the grooves are cut, rip the backs to width, cutting them flush to the top of the groove. Next, dovetail the drawers. Lay out the half pins on the drawer fronts. Set a marking gauge to ⁹⁄₁₆" and, from the inside face, mark the end grain on both ends of each drawer front.

Use the same setting to mark around the front of the drawer sides. Reset the marking gauge to the ³⁄₈" thickness of the drawer sides and mark the inside face on both ends of each front. With the same setting, also mark around the back of each side and around both ends of each drawer back. Lay out a ¼" half pin on the top and bottom of the drawer front and back. Also mark a ³⁄₈"-wide pin in the center. Mark the dovetail angle on the end grain and square the lines down the inside faces.

On the drawer fronts, saw at an angle, taking care not to cut through either marking gauge line, then chop out the waste, working down to the lap line on the fronts. Pare the pins until the cheeks are flat and perpendicular to the ends. Mark, cut, and fit the tails just as you did on the case.

Glue up the drawers, making sure they are square. Clean off all the

glue and flush all the surfaces with a handplane. Make sure the drawers sit flat on a flat surface. Test the drawer in its opening. Plane the top edges of the sides until the drawers move easily in their pockets.

### GLUE THE DRAWER STOPS

With the drawers fit, align the drawer fronts flush with the case and dividers. Apply a small amount of glue to each stop. Reach through the back of the case and position the stops on the tops of the dividers. Make sure the stop is tight to the back of the drawer front. Once the glue sets, test the drawer and trim the stop if necessary.

Cut the bottoms to fit in the grooves. Set the table saw to 6° with a zero-clearance insert and a featherboard in front of the blade. Set the fence to just under ¼" from the blade. Bevel both sides and the front of the bottom. Adjust the fence until the bottom just starts to slide into the drawer. Cut all of the bottoms and fine-tune the fit with a plane. When the bottoms fit, trim them flush to the back of the drawer. Cut a ½"-long x ⅛"-wide notch in the center of the back edge of each drawer bottom. Insert a screw through the notch into the drawer back to pinch and hold the bottom in place.

### SHIPLAP THE BACK

Rip the backboards to 4" wide. On one edge of each, cut a ³⁄₁₆"-deep x ³⁄₈"-wide rabbet. On two of the boards, cut the same rabbet on the opposite face of the opposite edge. Fit a single-rabbet board on the bottom of the case in the back rabbet and screw it along the bottom edge. Lay the double-rabbet boards in next so the rabbets overlap, leaving a ⅛" reveal in each joint. Screw these boards in at the ends, near where they overlap the board below. Trim the unrabbeted end of the final board until it fits in place with the same ⅛" reveal and screw it in place.

## SAND AND FINISH

Make sure all the glue has been cleaned off the surfaces. Address any tear out, dents, or gouges before you start to sand. Thoroughly sand; begin with #120-grit paper and progress through finer grits, stopping at #180 or #220 grit. Ease all the sharp edges. Apply the finish you prefer following the manufacturer's instructions. When it's dry, install drawer pulls of your choice (mine are iron; ¾" for the top drawers, 1⅛" for the bottom drawers).

When your toolbox is completed, you will have learned many of the essential woodworking skills. And if you're like me, your joinery tolerances will have tightened up a lot just learning the ins and outs of dovetailing. ◼

**EXPLODED VIEW**

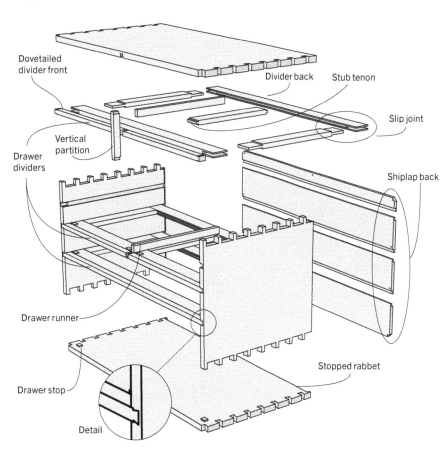

Dovetailed divider front

Divider back

Stub tenon

Slip joint

Vertical partition

Drawer dividers

Shiplap back

Drawer runner

Drawer stop

Stopped rabbet

Detail

**FRONT VIEW**

28"

⅝"  13⅛"  ½"

⅝"

1¾"

2"

13¼"

½"

2⅞"

3⅞"

½"

⅝"

**CROSS SECTION**

14½"

13¹¹⁄₁₆"

⅜"  ⅜"  ¾"

¼"

⅜"

⅝"

1¾"

½"

2"

12¾"

½"

2⅞"

½"

3⅞"

⅝"

# DUTCH TOOL CHEST

## This traditional traveling chest is faster and easier to build than a floor chest.

BY CHRISTOPHER SCHWARZ

Not everyone has the time, materials, or skills to build a full-scale traditional floor chest, which can have as many as 100 dovetails and banks of precisely fit sliding trays.

While I'm a fan of my large English tool chest, I've always been intrigued by the Dutch form. And after studying an authentic Dutch example owned by Roy Underhill, I decided to build a pair of these chests, try them out, and see how they worked.

The Dutch chests turned out to be a surprise at every turn. They are simple to build—each took me only two days of shop time, compared to the 40 to 60 hours needed to build a full-size English chest. They required much less material. And, most surprising of all, they were great chests both for the shop and on the road.

Now I won't lie to you, these Dutch chests aren't as sturdy or as good-looking as a quality floor chest. But they are stout enough; if you are short on time, materials, or skills, this might be the option for you.

### BUILT FOR SPEED

These Dutch chests—one small and one large—are built identically. The only difference is the large chest has an extra lower compartment. If you have a lot of tools—and I mean a lot—then build the large one. Otherwise, build the small one; it holds plenty.

Made from dimensional pine, the sides of the chest are 1x12s. These are dovetailed to the bottom board. The shelves are dadoed into the sides and then nailed with cut nails through the outside for good measure.

The front and back pieces are all attached to the carcase with screws and glue—if you use a dry softwood, then the wood won't move much in service and wood movement won't be a problem.

The lid is attached to the carcase with strap hinges and falls at a 30° angle. Some written accounts say this angle is to keep rain off the chest; others tout the angled lid as a place to do some paperwork on the job.

The fall-front is the most unusual part of the chest and bears some explanation. The fall-front has two battens that lip behind the bottom lip of the carcase—kind of like a primitive hinge. The front is held in place by a sliding piece of wood that threads through the carcase, through catches on the fall-front and

**Large or small.** To safeguard your tools, both versions of the Dutch tool chest feature fall-fronts with a resourceful and simple locking mechanism.

**Five easy pieces.** I think five tails on each side will be enough to hold the bottom, even with 100 pounds of stuff in the chest. Cut the joint however you please. I first gang-cut the tails on the sides and cut the pins second.

**Can't miss.** With a batten clamped to the work, even the longest dados (and sliding dovetails) are easy to cut with a handsaw or—shown here—a panel saw.

**Flat, smooth fit.** A router plane ensures that the bottom surface of the dado is flat. Be sure to remove the bulk of the waste with a chisel. Router planes take small bites.

back into a notch in the bottom of the chest.

The result is that when the lid is closed and locked, the fall-front cannot be removed. It's a clever precursor to the locking mechanism of machinists' tool chests.

### START WITH THE HARD PART

After cutting the chest's sides and bottom to length, begin the joinery by dovetailing the sides to the bottom. Cut the tails on the sides and the pins on the bottom—this will make the chest stronger overall, even if the glue fails.

After cutting the tails on the sides, transfer the layout to the bottom and cut the pins on the bottom board, then fit the joints.

### DADOS FOR THE SHELVES

The shelf or shelves for the chest are held in place with ¼"-deep dados in the sides of the chest. Lay out the shelf locations using the drawings as a guide. I typically cut this joint by hand without a guide for my saw. However, if this is your first hand-made dado, this is the easy way to do it:

Clamp a stout batten to the work and your bench that sits right on the line of your dado. Use a crosscut handsaw or panel saw to saw one wall of the dado by pressing the sawplate against the batten.

Don't remove the batten yet. First place the shelf against the batten and scribe the location of the other wall of the dado. Now reposition your batten onto that line, clamp it down, and saw the second dado wall. Remove the bulk of the waste between the walls with a chisel and finish the

**Keep the rain out.** You can make this saw cut with a batten—like you did with the dados. But try it freehand. This is an easy cut if you start at the far corner and nibble a kerf back toward you—then proceed with power strokes.

**Lock hardware?** These notches receive the sliding locks that thread through the carcase and the fall-front. Make the notches in the shelves as clean as you can—you'll be looking at them for a long time.

bottom of all the dados with a router plane. Make sure all your dados are the same depth, which will keep your chest square.

Once the dados are cut, plane the shelves to fit the dados, if necessary.

## SAW THE TOP
The sides of the chest are cut at a 30° angle. The best way to cut them is to clamp the sides together, lay out the angle, and then saw the angle with the pieces sandwiched together. I used a sash saw, though any crosscut saw will do the trick.

Once the sawcut is complete, keep the sides clamped together and plane away the sawblade marks. Confirm that your cut is 90° to the faces of the sides—adjust the cut with a plane if necessary.

## ASSEMBLE THE CARCASE
After a quick dry fit, apply glue to the dovetails and knock those cor-

ners together. Then put glue in the dados and drive in the shelves. Apply clamps across the shelves until the glue sets up. Then nail the shelves in place by driving 4d (1½") cut nails through the outside of the case and into the shelves. Set the nails. Confirm the carcase is square.

While the case is clamped up, cut the notches that will receive the sliding lock. I used two sliding locks for the large chest and one for the small one. The notches in the shelves are ¼" deep and 2" wide. The notches in the bottom are ¼" deep, 2" wide, and cut halfway through the thickness of the bottom. All the notches need to line up vertically for the locks to work.

Saw out as much waste as you can, then chop away the remainder with a chisel.

Once the notches are cut, screw the front, lower lip, and back onto the carcase. The lower lip is easy—just glue and screw. The front piece needs

A screw job. The backboards, front and bottom lip are all attached to the carcase with screws. This greatly speeds construction.

a 30° bevel on its top edge to match the 30° on the sides. The backboards should be shiplapped at the least (tongue-and-groove would be better). Then the top board of the back requires a 30° bevel on its top edge. Use #8 x 1¾" screws for the job.

The last bit of work on the carcase is to add the skids to the underside of the bottom. These disposable strips

of wood prevent the bottom from becoming rotten or worn quickly away. Screw the two skids to the bottom about 3" from the ends of the carcase. Bevel the corners of the skids to make the chest easier to drag.

**MAKE THE FALL-FRONT**

The removable fall-front of the Dutch chest is a cool feature. To make it work, you need to first fit the fall-front in its opening. Then you screw the battens to the backside of the fall-front. The battens do two things: They keep the fall-front flat through the long haul, and they grab onto the lower lip of the case to help keep the chest locked tight.

Screw the battens to the back of the fall-front so they protrude ½" beyond the bottom edge of the fall-front. Be sure to ream out the clearance holes for the screws in the battens to allow for a bit of seasonal wood movement.

### A CASE FOR BLACKSMITH HARDWARE

You can build this chest with almost any strap hinges—new or vintage. It's not a fussy project. But if you want to go all out, I suggest you look in your area for a blacksmith to make strap hinges and a hasp for you.

I used hardware from John Switzer of Black Bear Forge (blackbearforge.com). Yeah, they cost more than the off-the-rack stuff, but they look incredible.

Worth it. These strap hinges look about 2,000 times better than machine-made hinges. Once you use blacksmith-made hardware, it's difficult to go back.

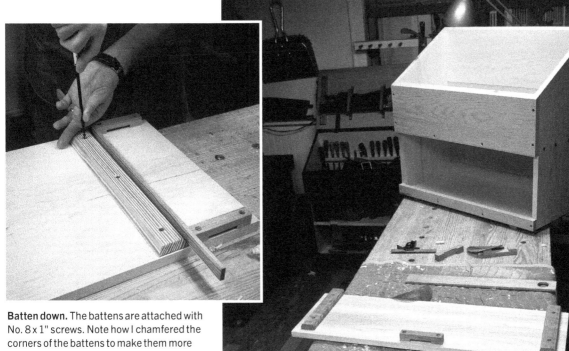

**Batten down.** The battens are attached with No. 8 x 1" screws. Note how I chamfered the corners of the battens to make them more friendly to fingers.

**Smaller bits.** Here you can see how the fall-front is simpler on the smaller chest.

Next you need to add the catches that will receive the sliding locks to the back of the fall-front. The catches are ¾" x ¾" x 4" and have a ½" x 2" notch cut in them to receive the sliding locks. You can add as many catches as you like, though one or two per sliding lock is sufficient.

Once you have the battens and catches screwed in place, you can make the sliding lock pieces. These are ¼"-thick x 2"-wide pieces of material (I used old pieces of heart pine). Thread them through all the notches and catches to make sure they fit. Cut them to final length so they are flush with the top of the front edge of the carcase. Then bore a 1"-diameter hole near the top of each sliding lock to make it easy for you to slide it out.

### DETAILS AND PAINT

You can trick out the chest as much as you like. I added a bead to a couple long edges. On the front of the fall-front, I planed a ⅛" deep, ½"-wide rabbet. On the lid, I added a thumbnail molding around three edges. There really are no hard-and-fast rules.

The lid itself can be fancy or plain. On the large Dutch chest, I screwed battens to the inside of the lid to keep it flat. On the smaller chest I used breadboard ends to help keep the lid flat.

The traditional finish for the exterior is paint. Most of the Dutch chests I've seen have been a chalky blue. I like black chests, so I used a black milk paint—not for its historic correctness but for its durability.

**That's catchy.** These little wooden bits receive the sliding locks as they slide down through the carcase. The more catches you have, the more secure the fall-front will be.

**CROSS SECTION: LARGE CHEST**

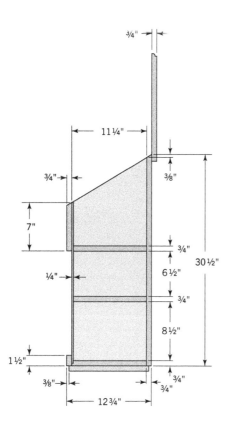

**FRONT VIEW: LARGE CHEST**

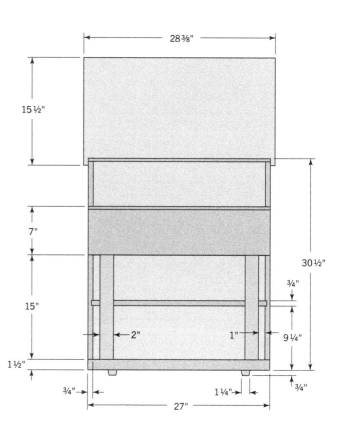

Strap hinges and a hasp will make the lid open and shut—and stay shut if you like. You can make your own wooden chest lifts to attach to the sides or buy metal ones.

### INTERIOR DETAILS

The real genius of the Dutch chest is how efficient the interior space is. The bottom compartments are sized perfectly for molding planes, rabbet planes, plows, and generally piling stuff. I don't recommend you break up this space into little compartments. Some Dutch chests would put a shallow drawer in this area, so that's an option to consider.

The top compartment is where you should have a tool rack for your chisels and other pointy tools—these racks are *de rigueur* on Dutch chests. I've experimented with lots of different racks through the years. What I prefer is a rack made from a 1" x 1" stick that is bored with ½"-diameter holes that are on 1⅛" centers. You'll have to widen a few of the holes for your wide chisels, but otherwise, it will hold many of your tools as-is.

The floor of the top compartment is ideal for holding your three bench planes—jack, jointer, and smoother—and your three joinery backsaws—dovetail, carcase, and

**3D VIEW: LARGE CHEST**

**3D VIEW: LARGE CHEST**

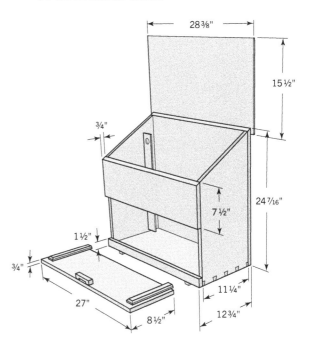

2"

Thin strip slides into notches in shelves and cleats in cover.

15"

4"

3/4"

1/2"

27"

15"

28 3/8"

15 1/2"

3/4"

24 7/16"

7 1/2"

1 1/2"

3/4"

27"

11 1/4"

8 1/2"

12 3/4"

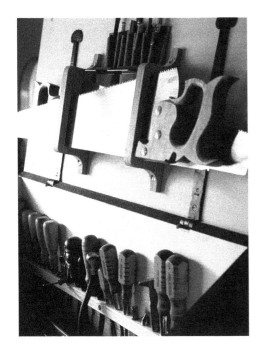

**Lid business (left).** You can cram a lot of stuff onto the lid if you think a little creatively. The saw till is simply made from bits of scrap that are glued together to allow the saw to slide in and out. Then I screwed them to the lid.

**Planes above (right).** The top compartment is large enough to hold your three bench planes and more— with ample space to add thin walls to keep the planes in place if you care to, and perhaps add a till for backsaws.

tenon. You can divide up the space with ¼"-thick walls that are tacked in place, or use an open floor plan.

The lid of the chest is a great place for holding two panel saws and, with a little creative leatherwork—all your marking tools.

How do you use this chest? I like to park it on a sawbench or chair by the workbench. I lift the lid and let it stay open. This setup give me easy access to all the tools in the chest without stooping.

What is most surprising about the chest is how easy it is to move around by myself. Unlike my English floor chest, I can lift this one easily by myself—it's only 130 pounds when fully loaded. And it fits in any car (even a two-door coupe). The only question mark in my mind about this chest is how long the whole thing will last. And I can promise I will find out—I use this chest almost every week when I'm on the road. ■

**The open plan.** The lower compartment is typically left open so you can stack or pile tools in as you see fit. I have been happy to leave it wide open because I can get more in there.

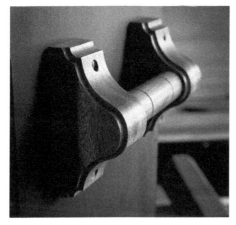

**Fancy or plain (left).** I made these mahogany lifts from scraps left over from another job. You also can buy simple chest lifts from the home center. You need lifts. Don't skip them.

**For security (right).** A hasp will keep the lid down and the sliding locks in place. Skip the hasp if you don't travel.

## CUT LIST & MATERIALS

| | NO. | ITEM | DIMENSIONS (INCHES) | | | MATERIAL | COMMENTS |
|---|---|---|---|---|---|---|---|
| | | | T | W | L | | |
| **LARGE CHEST** | | | | | | | |
| ☐ | 2 | Sides | ¾ | 11 ¼ | 30 ½ | Pine | Cut ¹⁄₁₆" oversize. |
| ☐ | 1 | Bottom | ¾ | 11 ¼ | 27 | Pine | Cut ¹⁄₁₆" oversize. |
| ☐ | 2 | Shelves | ¾ | 11 ¼ | 26 | Pine | In ¼"-deep dados. |
| ☐ | 1 | Front | ¾ | 7 | 27 | Pine | 30° bevel on top edge. |
| ☐ | 1 | Lower lip | ¾ | 1 ½ | 27 | Pine | |
| ☐ | 1 | Lid | ¾ | 15 ½ | 28 ⅜ | Pine | Back edge has 30° bevel to stay open. |
| ☐ | 2 | Skids | ¾ | 1 ¼ | 12 | Pine | |
| ☐ | 1 | Back | ¾ | 30 ½* | 27 | Pine | 30° bevel on one board's top edge. |
| ☐ | 1 | Fall-front | ¾ | 15 | 27 | Pine | |
| ☐ | 2 | Panel battens | ½ | 1 ½ | 15 | Pine | |
| ☐ | 4 | Catches | ¾ | ¾ | 4 | Pine | |
| ☐ | 2 | Lock strips | ¼ | 2 | 23 ⅛ | Pine | Cut long to fit cabinet. |
| **SMALL CHEST** | | | | | | | |
| ☐ | 2 | Sides | ¾ | 11 ¼ | 24 ⅞ | Pine | Cut ¹⁄₁₆" oversize. |
| ☐ | 1 | Bottom | ¾ | 11 ¼ | 27 | Pine | Cut ¹⁄₁₆" oversize. |
| ☐ | 1 | Shelf | ¾ | 11 ¼ | 26 | Pine | In ¼"-deep dados. |
| ☐ | 1 | Front | ¾ | 7½ | 27 | Pine | 30° bevel on top edge. |
| ☐ | 1 | Lower lip | ¾ | 1 ½ | 27 | Pine | |
| ☐ | 1 | Lid | ¾ | 15 ½ | 28 ⅜ | Pine | |
| ☐ | 2 | Skids | ¾ | 1 ¼ | 12 | Pine | |
| ☐ | 1 | Back | ¾ | 24 ⁷⁄₁₆* | 27 | Pine | 30° bevel on one board's top edge. |
| ☐ | 1 | Fall-front | ¾ | 8 ½ | 27 | Pine | Cut long to fit cabinet. |
| ☐ | 2 | Panel battens | ½ | 1 ½ | 8 | Pine | In ⅜" x ½" groove. |
| ☐ | 1 | Catch | ¾ | ¾ | 4 | Pine | ¼" roundover on one edge. |
| ☐ | 1 | Lock strip | ¼ | 2 | 17 ⅛ | Pine | Cut long to fit cabinet. |
| **SUPPLIES** | | | | | | | |
| ☐ | 2 | Strap hinges | | | | | |
| ☐ | 2 | Chest lifts | | | | | |
| ☐ | 1 | Hasp | | | | | |

* Width is composed of several tongue-and-groove boards.

**3**

# RACKS & CABINETS

**Mounted options will free up your floorspace.** This section is packed with tool racks and cabinets that get your tools up off the floor and onto the wall. Some designs are open for easy handle grabbing; others feature doors to keep out sawdust. Dividers, specialized shelves, and custom mounting brackets ensure the perfect place for every tool. Whether you need a new hangout for your chisels, saws, planes, router bits, or other tools, you'll soon have them cleanly mounted and within easy reach of your work zone.

# PORTABLE CHISEL RACK

## Keep your tools right where you need them.

BY CHRISTOPHER SCHWARZ

I've seen, used, and built a number of chisel racks, but none has ever seemed to suit me. Most of them are just a bit awkward.

And don't even get me started on the alternatives to a chisel rack: Chisel boxes and rolls take up too much valuable space on your bench, and keeping the chisels in the bench's tool tray just adds to the clutter that collects there.

What most woodworkers need is a rack that holds all their chisels upright where they can grab them. They need a rack that protects the sharp tips. And they need to be able to move the rack off the bench when they're assembling big projects there.

After months of sketches, we're sure we've got the perfect rack. It does everything we want it to do and it can be hung anywhere in the shop (on a bench, a wall, or even a cabinet side) thanks to a clever cleat.

And best of all, it's easy and fast to build with shop scraps.

## HOW DOES YOUR STEEL MEASURE UP?

The first thing to do is to measure a few dimensions on your chisels with a ruler and a dial caliper.

Find the thickest part of your thickest blade. Add 1/32" to that measurement and that will be the thickness of all the spacers between the chisels.

Measure the length of all of your chisels' blades and find the longest one. That length is the width of all of your spacers. (Yes, I do mean width. You want the grain of the spacers to run in the same direction as the front and back pieces.)

Then, measure the width of each chisel (don't assume that what is marked on the tool is correct). Add 1/16" to each measurement and that will determine the distance between each spacer. Take these measurements to the saw and rip a small piece of scrap to each of these widths. Mark them with their width. These scraps will help you place your spacers during assembly.

The spacers between each tool are 2 3/8" long. This might seem like a lot, but it allows you to grab any

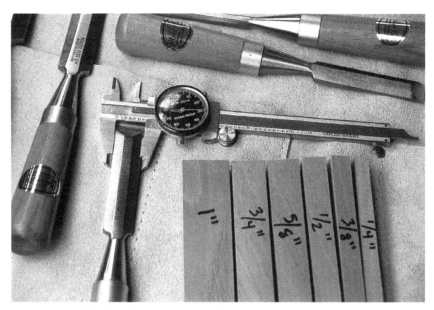

**Measure those chisels.** A dial caliper is handy for checking your chisels' dimensions. Measure the width of each blade, add 1/16" to each measurement, then rip a scrap piece to that width to help during assembly.

**Mark the layout.** Use those scrap pieces to lay out the location of the spacers on your back piece. When everything fits, glue and nail the spacers in place.

**The chamfer on the stop piece** and the slightly narrow front piece allow dust to escape the rack easily.

chisel without rapping your knuckles against its neighbor. Most chisel racks I've seen place the tools' handles too close together, so you're always fishing out the specimen you need.

## A CHISEL LASAGNA

This rack is essentially four layers of wood sandwiched together. You glue the spacers between the front and back pieces, then you screw a cleat to the back of the rack to hang it.

**FRONT VIEW (FRONT PIECE REMOVED)**

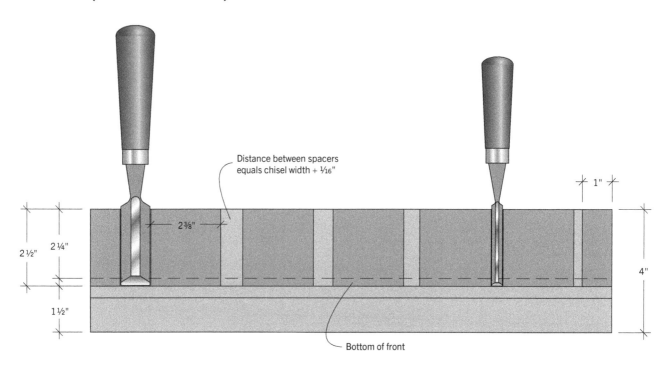

Distance between spacers equals chisel width + 1/16"

2 3/8"

1"

2 1/2"

2 1/4"

1 1/2"

4"

Bottom of front

**TOP VIEW**

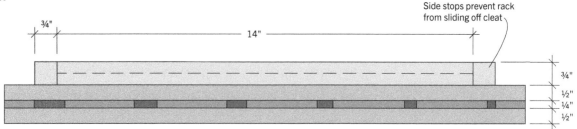

Side stops prevent rack from sliding off cleat

3/4"

14"

3/4"

1/2"
1/4"
1/2"

**SIDE VIEW**

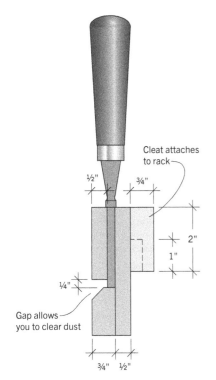

Cleat attaches to rack

½"  ¾"

2"
1"

¼"

Gap allows you to clear dust

¾"  ½"

**SIDE VIEW: CLEAT FOR WALL**

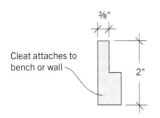

⅜"

Cleat attaches to bench or wall

2"

**Fit the cleats together.** A rabbet plane or shoulder plane makes quick work of the process. You want the cleat to fit tightly in the middle and a bit looser on the ends. This will allow you to pivot the chisel rack on and off its mating cleat.

The stop piece, which is located below the spacers, accomplishes two things: First, it keeps all the chisels at the same height. Second, it prevents you from destroying your rack.

Let's say you built the rack without the stop. Someday, you're going to accidentally drop something on one of your chisels in the rack. The chisel's socket will then wedge into the rack, splitting apart all your work. So spend the extra five minutes to cut and install the stop.

Now that you know the size of the spacers, the space that needs to go between them, and the lengths of the blades, you can calculate the dimensions of your front and back pieces (don't forget to add some width for the stop piece). You are ready to begin milling your wood.

Plane down all the pieces you'll need for the rack, then rip and crosscut all your pieces to size. The first step is to attach the stop piece to the back. But before you attach the stop,

## CUT LIST & MATERIALS

| | NO. | ITEM | DIMENSIONS (INCHES) | | | MATERIAL |
|---|---|---|---|---|---|---|
| | | | T | W | L | |
| ☐ | 1 | Back | ½ | 4 | 17¾* | Birch |
| ☐ | 1 | Front | ½ | 2¼ | 17¾* | Birch |
| ☐ | 2 | End spacers | ¼ | 2½† | 1 | Birch |
| ☐ | 5‡ | Spacers | ¼ | 2½† | 2⅜ | Birch |
| ☐ | 1 | Stop | ¾ | 1½ | 17¾* | Birch |
| ☐ | 1 | Cleat for rack | ¾ | 2 | 14* | Birch |
| ☐ | 1 | Cleat for wall or bench | ¾ | 2 | 13½§ | Birch |
| ☐ | 2 | Side stops | ¾ | ¾ | 2 | Birch |

\* Measurement equal to actual widths of all chisels plus 1 spacer between each and 2 end spacers. † Measurement equal to thickest tool plus ⅟₃₂". ‡ Number of spacers depends on the number of tools. § Measurement should be a few inches shorter than overall rack length.

cut a 45° chamfer on one long edge that measures ⅜" x ⅜". The chamfer makes it easier for dust that gets into the rack to fall out. Then glue the stop in place on the back.

Now nail one of the end spacers in place. Remember those scraps you ripped to width after you measured the width of your chisels? Get them. Place them between your spacers and make sure everything fits to your satisfaction. Now glue and nail the spacers (but not the scraps) in place using ½"-long brads.

When that's complete, glue the front piece to the spacers. You're almost done. Clean up all four edges of the assembled rack. Run the bottom edge over your jointer (or clean it up with a hand plane), then rip the rack to width on your table saw to clean up the top edge. Finally, crosscut the ends to tidy things up.

## A CLEVER CLEAT

This rack hangs anywhere using two cleats that interlock thanks to a ⅜"-deep x 1"-wide rabbet on each part. You want the fit between the two cleats to be firm. Here's how to do it right: Cut the rabbet on one long edge of each cleat so it's just a touch shy of ⅜" deep, maybe by a few thousandths.

Screw one of the cleats to your bench, shop wall, or cabinet. With the other cleat, plane or sand the rabbet at the ends so that the surface is a very gentle and subtle curve. Break the sharp corners of the joint using a block plane or sandpaper, which will make nesting the two cleats easier.

Screw (but don't glue) this cleat to your rack and give it a try. If the fit is too tight, remove the cleat and thin down the rabbet a bit more. If the fit is too loose, remove the cleat and make a few passes with a plane on the area where the cleat attaches to the rack. This will tighten up the fit.

Once you're satisfied, glue and nail the two side stops on either end of the cleat that's attached to the rack. The side stops will prevent you from pushing the rack off its cleat.

Sand, plane, or scrape the surfaces of the rack and add a clear finish. Finish your rack with whatever you used on your workbench. For me it's a wiping varnish comprised of three parts varnish and one part paint thinner.

Since I've installed this rack, I've been astonished at how many trips it has saved me to hunt down the chisel I'm looking for. This rack's a keeper. ■

# TOOL RACK

## Swiped from a French engraving, this rack works in the shop or even in your kitchen.

BY CHRISTOPHER SCHWARZ

It's good to keep your tools protected (think: tool chest). But it's also good to heep them handy (think: at arm's reach). My favorite way to accomplish both goals is a stout tool rack.

I've made many tool racks since I became a woodworker, most of them crude affairs that were cobbled together in a few minutes. I've always wanted a rack that both looks good and is easy to build. Then, while

browsing a French book on vintage handplanes, I saw it.

In a 19th-century engraving of a French workshop, the back wall was covered with a rack very much like this one. Finding it and drawing it to scale were the hard parts. Building it took just a few hours.

### YOU KNOW THE DRILL

The project is assembled using pocket screws, dimensional pine, and some

**SIDE VIEW**

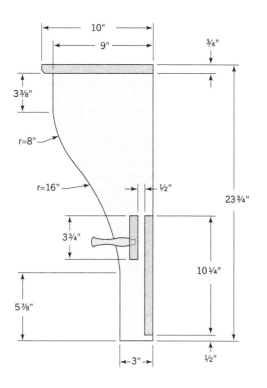

Shaker pegs I found at our home center (will wonders never cease?).

You are going to need at least 12' of 1x12 and 4' of 1x4 pine to build this rack. Once you have the wood in hand, the first step is to cut all the parts to length. Then rip the back and top pieces to width. Use a circular saw with an edge guide to make the rips, or use a jigsaw to make the rips and then remove the saw blade marks with your block plane.

Next, work on the ogee shape of the ends. I used SketchUp to create a full-size paper template. I stuck the paper to one of the end pieces using spray adhesive. I cut the ogee shape using a jigsaw and cleaned up the curves with a rasp and sandpaper. Then, I used the finished end piece as a pattern to make the second end.

**FRONT VIEW**

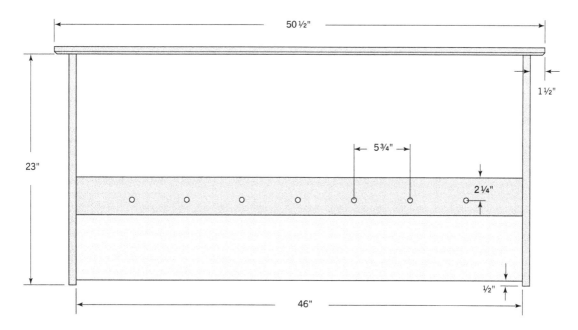

## EVERYTHING IS IN POCKET

All the joinery for this rack is screws. Bore three pocket holes on each end of the 1x4, which is the front of the tool rack. Drill five pocket holes on each end of the back piece of the rack.

You are just about ready to assemble the bulk of the rack, but first clean off all the tool marks using a block plane or sandpaper.

You have to assemble the rack's parts in a certain way for everything to go together. The first job is to screw the front 1x4 to the end pieces.

The position of this part is critical because it will determine how much of a gap you will have between the front and the back of your rack. And this gap is what holds your tools. After much experimentation, I have found that a ½" gap is ideal for handling about 99 percent of my tools. However, you should take a close look at the tools you are going to store on your rack before you imitate me.

Use my drawing (or your own modified drawing) to mark a line where this front piece will join the ends. Clamp the front piece in position and screw it down. Screw the other end in place using the same procedure.

Screw the back piece in place. You should be able to squeeze it between the two ends, tap it gently in place, then screw it tightly to the ends.

Now you can turn your attention to the top piece. I cut a ¼" x ¼" chamfer on the underside of the top using a block plane. This is easy to do free-hand—just use your combination square to lay out the pencil lines for the chamfer and plane the corner down to them. A little irregularity is OK.

**Screw this.** The entire project is assembled with pocket screws. Here I'm boring five pocket holes on one end of the back piece.

**Stops sagging.** Don't forget the little L-brackets under the top. These prevent the top piece from sagging.

## CUT LIST & MATERIALS

| | NO. | ITEM | DIMENSIONS (INCHES) | | | MATERIAL |
|---|---|---|---|---|---|---|
| | | | T | W | L | |
| ☐ | 2 | Ends | ¾ | 9 | 23 | 1x12 pine |
| ☐ | 1 | Back | ¾ | 10 ¼ | 46 | 1x12 pine |
| ☐ | 1 | Front | ¾ | 3 ¾ | 46 | 1x4 pine |
| ☐ | 1 | Top | ¾ | 10 | 50 ½ | 1x12 pine |
| ☐ | 8 | Shaker pegs | | | | Pine |
| ☐ | 2 | L brackets | | | | |

The top of the rack is screwed to the ends. It's not done with pocket holes—just six simple countersunk #8 x 1¼" wood screws.

### I'VE GOT YOU PEGGED

The Shaker pegs on the front of the rack give you more places to hang your tools. The seven pegs are spaced every 5 ¾" across the front of the rack. The center of each hole is 2¼" down from the top edge of the front of the rack.

The pegs I bought needed ½"-diameter and ½"-deep holes. Drill the holes, dab in some glue and knock them home. I had an extra peg left over from the package from the home center and put it on one of the ends to hold my shop apron (our photographer hung a backsaw on it for the photo on p. 125).

### FINISHING AND HANGING

My first instinct was to paint this rack, but the pine I found was clear enough to use without paint. So the finish for this rack is the same I use for all my shop furniture. I thin down satin spar varnish with paint thinner at 3:1. I wipe on three coats, sanding between each coat with a #320-grit sanding sponge.

Hanging the rack is simple. Find the studs in your shop wall. Drive #8 x 3" screws through the back of the rack and into your studs. Then purchase two simple L brackets. Screw them to the underside of the top and into your studs. That should do the trick.

Though this rack is intended for the shop, several people who have seen it insist they are going to build one for the kitchen and put their knives in the rack, hang pots on the pegs, and put cookbooks on the top shelf. As the French are both expert craftsmen and chefs, this is entirely appropriate. ■

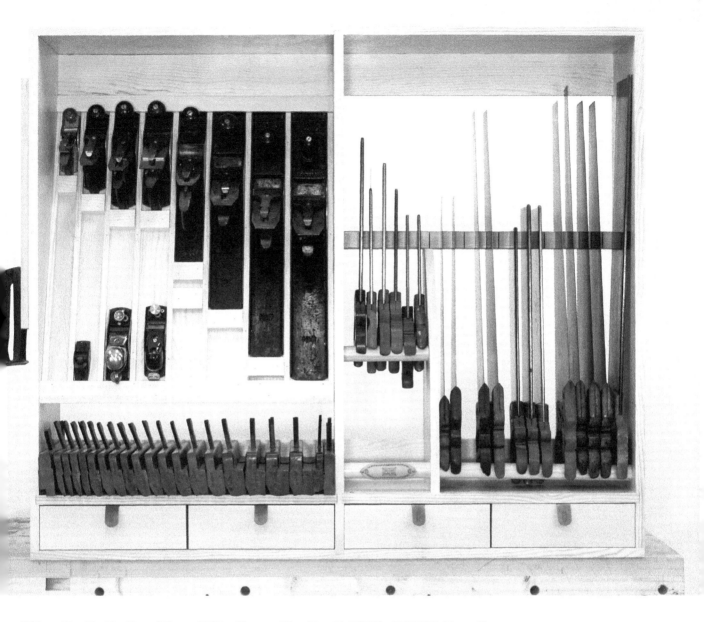

# SAW & PLANE TILL

**It won't solve a tool addiction, but it'll make finding tools easier.**

BY MIKE SIEMSEN

You've no doubt seen photos of the H.O. Studley tool cabinet—the Sistine Chapel of tool cabinets. And as far as I'm concerned, Studley got it right. Yes, his tool chest is a work of art and all that, but more importantly, it hangs on the wall.

With apologies to all you people who love floor chests, I prefer wall-hung tool storage if I don't have to travel and I have the wall space. I can see at a glance where my tools are and I find my access is easier.

This saw and plane till is open for easy access, but with a few modifications you could put doors on it to keep out humidity (or co-workers). It's also a simple matter to add a back.

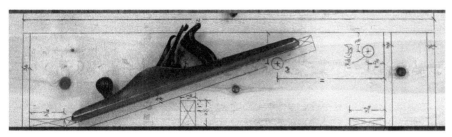

**Bespoke fit.** You can get an exact fit for your tools if you use them as the basis for your till's measurements.

### FIRST, ADMIT THE PROBLEM

I designed this till for my minion, Tod Twist (we don't have apprentices any more). Tod needed tool storage, and I needed fodder for an article.

Because you're reading a woodworking book, it's probably safe to assume that you have a saw or plane problem (or both).

This till holds 21 saws, the Stanley bench planes from No. 1 to No. 8, and a half set of hollows and rounds. It has four drawers to store parts and sharpening equipment, saw sets, files, and the like. I hang my saw vise from a nail in the side.

You can build just the saw till or the plane till, or combine them as we did. Feel free to make it wider or narrower as your needs dictate.

You can also omit the drawers. Be sure to leave "room for growing" like my mother did when she bought me clothes and shoes when I was a boy.

### MADE TO FIT

We decided on lumberyard pine for our project. At first, Tod thought it was "curly pine" but then he realized it was just knife marks from the planer. We used 1x10 material, which made the case 9 5/16" deep after assembly.

I started by placing my longest saw on a board and marking the location of the dowel the totes would rest on, as well as where I thought the slotted separator that holds the sawplates should go.

From panel saw to half-rip to miter saw, I placed several saws on the drawing to ensure the placement worked for most saws. I did the same for the location of a higher dowel to hold shorter backsaws.

I used my longest plane to set the length of the plane till and work out the location of the rabbeted top cleat and the bottom cleat that the planes rest on.

I drew everything on the same board; the parts for the plane till are easy to tell apart from the parts for the saw till.

The outer case is joined with through-dovetails and dadoed for the shelves and divider.

### START CUTTING

Once you are sure of your dimensions, cut your outside pieces to length.

Using a saw, chisel, and router plane, Minion Tod and I cut 1/4"-deep dados in the sides, top, and bottom. Then we cut 1/8"-deep dados in either side of the center divider to hold the shelf pieces.

Cut the vertical rod support piece that will hold the short dowel rod and notch it for a hanging cleat. Make the same notches on the two ends and the center divider. When I hang a case like this, I just screw through the cleats and into the wall, but you could add a French cleat if you go for that sort of thing.

Now cut the dovetails, but be sure to remember the 3/4" x 3 1/2" notch for the hanging cleat when you lay out the dovetails at the top. The pins for the dovetails should be on the top and bottom boards for easier assembly.

Bore the holes for the dowels that will hold the saw handles. Lay out and drill 1¼"-diameter blind holes ½" deep in the divider and rod support piece for the short dowel; do the same in the divider and case side for the long dowel. Drill a through-hole in the rod support for the long dowel.

Cut the long dowel to length (it should be 1" longer than the opening). Cut the two hanging cleats to length (they should be the width of the case).

Sand the inside of the case to clean it up a bit, and you are ready to assemble. And go wash your hands—you don't want to dirty up your sanded parts.

## GET IT TOGETHER

Begin assembly by inserting one of the shelves into the dado in the center divider and drive a 6d nail through the opposite side of the dado. Insert the other shelf and fasten it with a 6d finishing nail driven from the bottom face of the first shelf. Angle the nails and set them with a nail set.

Center and attach the bottom cleat to the shelves with 8d nails driven from the bottom face of the shelf into the cleat. Drive a 2" screw into the divider from the back of the cleat.

Center and nail the top cleat to the back edge of the top with 8d nails. Make sure you nail through the upper face of the top piece, or your dovetail pins and dado will be in the wrong orientation.

Insert the center divider into the dado in the top and screw the top to the divider with 1⅝" screws. Using 2" screws, attach the cleat to the divider.

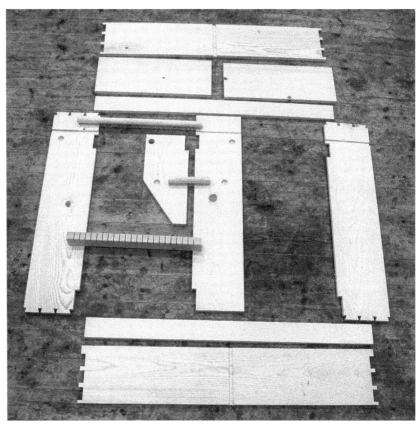

**Assembly required.** This exploded view of the till's components shows the blind holes for the support rods; the dados; and the saw separator.

Insert the center divider into the dado in the bottom board and attach it with 1⅝" screws.

Slide the long rod through the rod support and insert the dowel into the lower blind hole in the center divider.

Apply glue to your dovetails and fit the ends to the top and bottom, making sure the rod goes into its blind hole and the shelf into its dado. Screw the side to the shelf with 1⅝" screws. Drive 2" screws through the hanging cleats into the sides. Square up the case and let the glue dry.

## SAW SEPARATOR

While the glue is drying, make the saw separator from a tight-grained

2x4. It should be the same length as the width of the opening it fits into.

Because saw handles are typically ⅞" thick, make the notches 1" on center. The notches are ⅛" wide and 1" deep. I used a powered miter saw for this because the blade cuts a ⅛"-wide kerf and has a depth stop.

Slide the rod support over to the divider and mark it at the top to locate the position of the saw separator; slide it over to the side and do the same.

Place the separator where you want it, leaving the number of slots you think you will need on either side of the rod support. Attach the separator with a 2" screw through the divider and the case side.

Measure and cut your short rod to 1" longer than the opening (because the blind holes are ½" deep). We used 8", giving us a 7" opening for Tod's backsaws.

The rod support will center on a saw slot. To attach it, screw up through the shelf into the rod support and through the hanging cleat with a 2" screw and down through the separator with a 3" screw. If you decide to change the location of the rod support later, you can take out

the screws and move it to where you want. You'll need to make another short rod or cut off the short rod you have, depending on which way you move the rod support.

Take a step back and admire your work! Enjoy a cool beverage and look around your shop, put some things away and tidy up a bit; savor your life.

Enough of that, get back to work!

## NICE DRAWERS

For your drawer fronts, pick a nice ¾"-thick board the width of your case and the height of the drawer opening.

Cut four equal-sized drawer fronts from this board, allowing about ¹⁄₁₆" between the fronts in each opening. (After planing the sides, there will be a bit more play.)

Keep your drawers in order so the grain will match along the fronts when the drawers are installed.

The drawers are dovetailed at the corners with the bottoms nailed on.

The sides and back of the drawers are ½"-thick material and are ¼" narrower than the opening and your drawer fronts. The bottoms are ¼" thick, the same width as the drawer front and ¼" narrower than the total depth of the drawer.

The drawer backs are the same length as the front. Each drawer side is ¼" less than the drawer depth.

We gang-cut the tails in the sides and cut half-blind dovetails in the fronts and through-dovetails in the back.

Cut a ½" by ¼"-wide rabbet in the bottom back edge of the drawer front to receive the ¼"-thick bottom. Glue and nail the bottoms on each drawer using ⅞" nails and setting the heads below the surface.

**Matched set.** Use a single board for your drawer fronts to keep the grain matching across your till.

## CUT LIST & MATERIALS

| | NO | ITEM | DIMENSIONS (INCHES) | | | MATERIAL |
|---|---|---|---|---|---|---|
| | | | T | W | L | |
| ☐ | 2 | Sides | ¾ | 9 5/16 | 42 | Pine |
| ☐ | 1 | Divider | ¾ | 9 5/16 | 41 | Pine |
| ☐ | 2 | Top/bottom | ¾ | 9 5/16 | 50 | Pine |
| ☐ | 2 | Hanging cleats | ¾ | 3 ½ | 50 | Pine |
| ☐ | 1 | Long dowel | 1 ¼-dia. | | 24 ⅞ | Closet rod |
| ☐ | 1 | Short dowel | 1 ¼-dia. | | 8 | Closet rod |
| ☐ | 1 | Saw separator* | 1 ½ | 2 ½ | 23 ⅞ | Pine |
| ☐ | 1 | Rod support | ¾ | 9 5/16 | 19 5/8 | Pine |
| ☐ | 2 | Shelves | ¾ | 9 5/16 | 24 ¼ | Pine |
| ☐ | 1 | Plane till panel | ¾ | 23 ⅞ | 26 9/16 | Pine |
| ☐ | 2 | Plane till cleats† | ¾ | 1 ½ | 23 ⅞ | Pine |
| ☐ | 2 | Plane till battens | ¾ | 2 ¾ | 23 ⅞ | Pine |
| ☐ | 8 or 9 | Plane dividers | ½ | ½ | 24 | Pine |
| ☐ | 7 or 8 | Plane blocks | ¾ | 1 ½ | ‡ | Pine |
| ☐ | 4 | Drawer fronts | ¾ | 3 ¼ | 11 5/8 | Pine |
| ☐ | 8 | Drawer sides | ½ | 3 | 8 5/16 | Pine |
| ☐ | 4 | Drawer backs | ½ | 3 | 11 5/8 | Pine |
| ☐ | 4 | Drawer bottoms | ¼ | 8 5/16 | 11 5/8 | Pine |

* 1" notches, ⅛" wide, spaced 1" apart. † One cleat has a ½" x ½" rabbet. ‡ Blocks should match the width of the plane slot opening.

The grain in the bottom runs the same direction as the grain in the drawer front. Be sure to glue the front lip of the drawer to the bottom so it doesn't break off.

After the glue dries, plane the sides to clean them up and fit them to the case. While you're at it, plane to clean up the dovetails on the case.

### THE RIGHT ORDER

Be sure to number your drawers so they will go back in the proper order. I like to use Roman numerals at the top edge of the drawer front.

A single chisel strike is a I; a double strike II; and so on. Look at a clock dial if you get stuck. (By the way, there are II kinds of people in the world: those who can read Roman numerals and those who can't.)

The drawer stops and drawer guides are actually four nails. To make the drawer stops and guides, first drill pilot holes and drop an 8d headed nail that is snipped to about 1¼" long through the shelf next to the divider at the inside edge of the drawer at the front corner. Then make similar holes through the shelf next to the carcase sides.

Put the nails about ¾" from the front edge and about 9/16" in from the verticals, where they will act as stops and rude guides for the drawers. To remove a drawer, just pull out the nail.

**FRONT VIEW**

**LEFT CROSS SECTION**

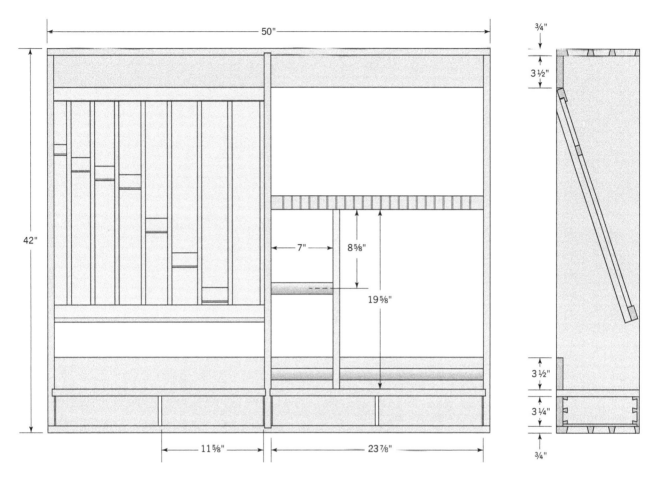

Tod is a leather worker, so he made leather pulls for his drawers and stamped them with his maker's mark.

### PLANE TILL

Construct the plane till so it is the width of your opening and the length of the longest plane it will hold, plus 2 9/16".

Refer to your drawing to see how much of an angle to put on the top back edge to create more clearance for the till.

Our plane till is just under 24" wide after assembly, so we used three pine

**Organic form.** Tod created leather pulls and stamps, complete with his mark, for this till—exercise your creativity and make your till your own.

**RIGHT CROSS SECTION**

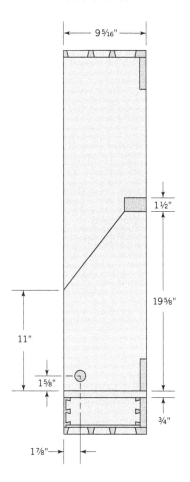

9 5/16"

1 1/2"

19 5/8"

11"

1 5/8"

3/4"

1 7/8"→

**DRAWER DETAIL**

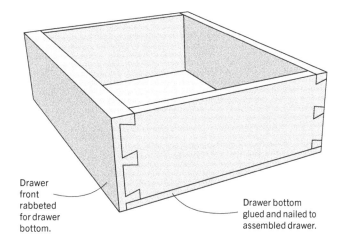

Drawer front rabbeted for drawer bottom.

Drawer bottom glued and nailed to assembled drawer.

boards, ¾" thick x 8" wide. The boards could be splined or joined tongue-and-groove, but we just butted ours together without glue.

Attach the top notched cleat (1½"x ¾" with a ½" x ½" rabbet) in the corner of the front face with some glue and small nails. Orient it with the rabbet on the lower back of the cleat, giving the plane toes a convenient retention lip. Set your longest plane in place and attach the bottom front cleat in the same way, leaving about ¹⁄₁₆" to ease moving the plane in and out.

Flip the panel over and attach the 2¾" x ¾" back batten to the panel with

1¼" screws. The upper batten should be low enough that it doesn't stick out past the back and contact the wall when installed. The bottom batten is nailed flush to the bottom edge.

Fit the plane till in place with its top against the top hanging cleat and the bottom just behind the cabinet's front face. Mark around the ends with a pencil so you can locate your screw holes, then remove the panel.

Drill through the divider and the end inside the lines so the screws will go into the boards of the till. Three 2" screws per side should be plenty, with one screw 2" from each end and one in the center. You might need to move the screw locations around to avoid problems with saw till pieces on the other side of the divider.

**STICKING STICKS**

Make up a batch of square sticks to use as dividers for your planes—the number depends on the level of your plane-buying problem. The sticks need to fit under the rabbet in the top cleat, so they will be just under ½" square.

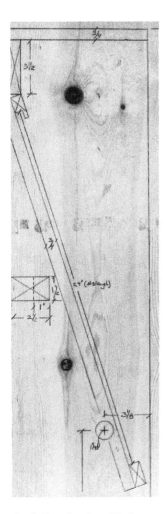

**Lean back.** Your drawing will help you determine the best angle for your plane till for both clearance and good looks.

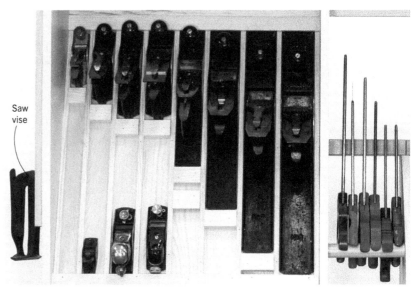

**Ruler trick.** A ruler and a few sticks are all you need to set the spacing between your planes.

Using small nails, attach one stick to each outside corner of the till.

Set your longest plane in place, put a ruler between the plane body and the next stick, then attach the stick.

Repeat the process for your next plane, using the plane and ruler to set the width. Next, cut a 1½" x ¾" block the width of the spacing (a plane plus ruler thickness) and nail that block in place below your plane, leaving just a bit of room to ease removing and replacing the plane.

If you have wooden planes, make a taller rabbeted block for the top and screw it to the till.

All of this is easier to do if you lay the till on its back.

Our opening just happened to be the right width to put in each plane from No. 1 through No. 8 so it looked nice for the photo.

**ALMOST DONE**

Give everything a light sanding and a coat of your favorite finish. We used clear shellac.

While the finish is drying, figure out how high the bottom of the cabinet should be from the floor.

Cut two pieces of 2x4 to that length, then locate your studs. Get a helper and set your cabinet on the 2 x 4s; have your helper hold the cabinet against the wall so it can't fall forward or move side to side. Drive 3" to 4" screws through the hanging cleat and into the studs.

After completing the till, we got the same question from several people. What goes in the space under the short backsaws? This is your own personal space, a place for your Chris Schwarz commemorative bobble-head from Woodworking in America 2004, first-aid supplies, your favorite emergency beer, or just pile it full of marking gauges.

For me, it is a shrine for my St. Roy action figure complete with sharp tools and a wound that bleeds. ■

# ROY UNDERHILL'S NAIL CABINET

It's a crate. It's a cabinet. It's useful shop furniture.

BY CHRISTOPHER SCHWARZ

One of the enduring features of Roy Underhill's *The Woodwright's Shop* PBS television show is the familiar and rambling backdrop of former projects, parts, tools, and wood that frames most episodes. My favorite item in his shop is his nail cabinet—a pine wall-hung cabinet tucked in the far back corner.

On the inside of the door of the cabinet, Roy has hung a print of a lovely lady holding a bock beer alongside an admiring goat. And while that's some nice lens candy for the television cameras, I'm more attracted to the 21 drawers on the right side of the cabinet. These draw-

ers are more useful to the married woodworker.

Nail cabinets show up frequently in traditional workshops of many trades, and they are illustrated and discussed in books about traditional shops. These cabinets stored the screws, nails, and bolts that a workshop might need. And because these fasteners were valuable, many of the cabinets would have a lock.

The last time I visited Roy, I asked permission to measure and reproduce his nail cabinet, which he purchased from a yard sale in Washington, D.C. As I measured the piece, I was bemused by its unusual

**EXPLODED VIEW**

construction—it was a finger-jointed carcase covered in nailed-on battens.

Then Roy showed me the reason for the odd construction: The cabinet was built from an old crate for Ohio Blue Tip Matches made by the Ohio Match Co. of Wadsworth, Ohio (1895–1987). For me, this made the project even more fun: I had to first build a crate and then turn it into a wall cabinet.

As a result, some of the construction techniques might seem a bit odd. If you don't like them, feel free to change them. My goal was to make a respectable reproduction of this charming cabinet because I've always liked the one on Roy's show.

## CONSTRUCTION OVERVIEW

The original is made entirely of pine—probably eastern white pine— though any dry softwood will do. The carcase of the original crate is joined at the corners with finger joints (though I opted for dovetails on my version). The back of the carcase is nailed-on ⅜"-thick boards that are shiplapped.

The assembled carcase is covered with narrow 1x battens to make the "crate" easy to grab and lift. These battens conceal the joinery on the corners of the carcase.

Once you have your "crate" built, you can turn it into a cabinet. The interior is divided into 21 spaces using thin pieces of pine that are joined with an egg-crate joint. The drawers are simply glued and nailed together; the only thing difficult about the drawers is that you have to build 21 of them.

Finally, the entire cabinet is fronted by a door with mitered cor-

**Gang-cut tails.** Whenever possible, I gang-cut my tail boards, which saves time and (in my opinion) makes it easier to keep the saw 90° to the face of the board. A shallow rabbet on each tail board makes it easy to keep things square during transfer.

**As square as possible.** Take extra pains to get the carcase square at glue-up. It will save you frustration later when you fit the door and the 21 drawers.

**Hide the gap.** The shiplapped joints on the long edges of the backboards hide any gap that would open up when the boards shrink in the dry season.

**Nails, no glue.** Nails will bend, allowing the back to expand and contract without splitting the backboards. Be sure to use nails with a pronounced head to hold the backboards in place.

ners. The panel of the original door was simply nailed to the inside of the mitered door frame. The panel had cracked over time, so I chose to make my panel float in grooves plowed into the rails and stiles.

The whole thing is finished with shellac and hung on the wall with a French cleat.

## THE WALLS OF THE CRATE

As mentioned above, the walls of the original crate were joined at the corners by narrow finger joints (you

**More gang-cutting.**
Lay out the slots on
one board, clamp
all the dividers
together, and make
the cut in one go.
Here on the table
saw, I'm using the
saw's miter gauge
and a high fence to
push the dividers
through the blade.

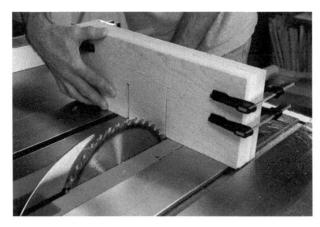

**Friction and pins.**
You should have
to knock the joints
together with a
mallet. Then pin all
the intersections
with 1"-long head-
less brads. You'll
have to nail them in
diagonally to secure
them.

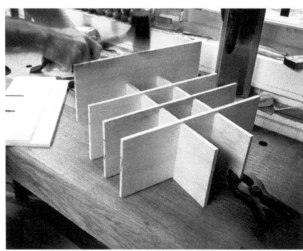

**Nailing jig.** This
scrap-wood jig
helps you locate
exactly where the
horizontal dividers
are located. It is
made using two thin
pieces of scrap that
are nailed to a scrap
of ½"-thick pine.
Slip the jig onto the
carcase and press
one of the thin slips
against the dividers
inside the case.
Trace its location
on the exterior.
Repeat.

can see the joints from the inside
where they have separated a bit). I
don't have the jigs or desire to make
narrow finger joints here, and cutting
this machine joint by hand is just
silly.

So I joined the case sides, top, and
bottom using through-dovetails. The
joinery is all covered by battens in the
end, so the end result looks the same
as the original. For strength, I put the
tails on the case sides; the pins are on
the top and bottom bits.

Glue up the carcase, paying close
attention to keeping the corners
square at both the front and rear of
the case. I use hide glue for joints like
this because it's reversible.

If you can't get the case perfectly
square at glue-up, you have one
more chance to pull it square with
the backboards. The backboards
are ⅜"-thick boards of pine that are
shiplapped on their long edges and
nailed to the back of the case. I used
3d cut fine finish standard nails to
affix the back, though 4d will do.

If your case is out of square, pull
the case square with a clamp diagonally across two corners, then nail
the backboards in place. This usually
helps if the case isn't too racked.

### THE INTERIOR DIVIDERS
The interior drawer dividers of the
original nail cabinet were obviously
built up using miscellaneous scraps
that were nailed and glued on to get
the job done. Some parts were rough-
sawn; some were different species.

Instead of replicating every odd
scrap in the cabinet, I simplified the
construction while still maintaining
its look and function. On the original,
the horizontal and vertical dividers

are joined with egg-crate joints, and so I used that same joint for my dividers.

The dividers are all ⅜" thick and 6" wide. Every divider has ⅜"-wide slots cut into it. The slots on the horizontal dividers are 2⅞" long. The slots on the vertical dividers are 3" long. When the dividers are knocked together, they will be offset by ⅛" at the front, just like the original.

Lay out the locations of all the slots using the drawings as a guide. I used dividers to step off the drawer sizes, and I used an actual piece of the drawer divider to lay out the width of the slots. Note that the three bottom drawers are taller than the others.

I cut the slots on a table saw, though they are easy to cut by hand or on a bandsaw. After cutting the slots, knock the dividers together and pin the joints by toenailing them with headless brads.

With the dividers together, knock the assembly into the carcase. The front edge of the horizontal dividers should be located 1½" from the front edge of the carcase. That spacing allows room for the bin pulls and knobs on the drawers.

The next step is to nail the horizontal dividers to the carcase. This is done easily with a simple jig that makes it (almost) impossible to miss with your nails. (See the bottom photo on p. 140 for details on the jig.)

Use 4d headless brads to secure the horizontal dividers to the carcase. There's no need to nail the vertical dividers to the carcase; gravity and friction are sufficient.

## MAKING IT A CRATE

The fun part of this project is taking this nice carcase and turning it into a

**Affix the dividers.** With the lines drawn on the carcase sides, drive in the cut headless brads and set them ¹⁄₁₆" below the surface.

**Piece by piece.** The battens form the rails and stiles that frame the exterior walls of the crate. As on the original, they are simply nailed and glued to the carcase—there's no joinery between the rails and stiles. So this is fast work.

packing crate. You do this by nailing on 1x battens so they look a bit like rails and stiles. There is no other joinery between the battens—just glue and nails.

Cut the battens to the sizes shown in the cutlist. The easy way to install these is to first attach them to the

**Inaccurate (top).** The 45° setting on my iron miter box is off by about half a degree. But I don't mind. That's because I shoot my miters, which allows me to sneak up on the perfect length and angle.

**Nail the miters (bottom).** A single nail through the stile and into the rail prevents things from sliding around as you clamp up this mitered joint. This was, by the way, how the original door was assembled.

carcase sides, trim the pieces flush to the top and bottom of the case, then finish up the work on the top and bottom.

The important thing to remember is that the battens should extend out ½" (or a tad more) from the front lip of the carcase. This ½" lip creates the opening for the door. Before you attach the battens, make sure their position works with the hinges you have purchased for the door. If the hinge leaf is wider than ½" you have to shift the battens forward a little on the case so the hinge can open and close. All the battens are attached with brads and glue.

## MITERED DOOR

With all the battens attached, you can determine the final sizes of your rails and stiles for the frame-and-panel door. The corners are joined by miters that are glued and nailed, just like the original.

When I cut miters, I saw them first, then trim them to a perfect length and a perfect 45° with a miter shooting board and a handplane.

Even if you love your chop saw, I encourage you to give this a try sometime. I've found no easier way to cut perfect miters. By shooting the miters with a handplane, you can control the length of your rails and stiles in .001" increments. And you can hit dead-on 45° with ease.

Once the miters are cut, plow a ³⁄₁₆"-wide x ³⁄₁₆"-deep groove on the inside edge of the rails and stiles. The ³⁄₈"-thick panel fits into the groove thanks to a rabbet cut on all four edges of the panel. Be sure to size the panel so it has a little room for expansion and contraction in its width.

**Begin with the bottom.** Get each bottom board to slide in and out of its opening before sizing the other drawer parts. If the bottom binds, the assembled drawer will bind.

**Glue the bottom.** Because the parts are all softwood, which doesn't move much once it's dry, you can get away with both gluing and nailing this cross-grain joint.

**Too long?** Dry assemble the drawer to feel if the drawer front is too long.

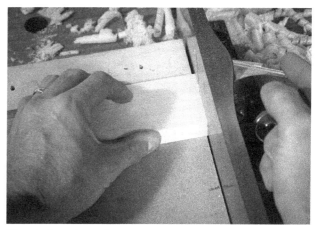

**Shoot it.** If the drawer front is too long, shoot it to perfect length with a plane on a shooting board. Count your strokes. Reduce the length of the drawer back by the same number of strokes, provided your original lengths were the same.

I don't own any fancy clamps for gluing mitered corners—most band clamps are fairly frustrating to use—so I glue up miters corner by corner.

First, I spread a little glue on the two mating surfaces of the miter and let them dry for a minute. I add more glue to the joint. I press the two pieces together and drive a single nail through the stile and into the rail.

I repeat this for each corner (don't forget to slide the panel into the frame before adding the last piece). Then, I clamp the joints using four bar clamps. The nails prevent the miters from sliding as you apply pressure.

**TWENTY-ONE DRAWERS**

Because this is a cabinet for nails, it's appropriate that the drawers are nailed together. All the drawers are constructed in a simple manner: The front and back are captured by the sides. The bottom is then nailed on.

The drawers look a little odd—the end grain of the sides and bottom is visible on the drawer front. But they are acceptable for a piece of shop furniture—and the drawers in the original have survived many years of use.

Begin by fitting all the drawer parts for each opening. I try to do as much fitting as I can before assembly so the drawer will require little or no tweaking afterward. First, I fit each bottom to its opening. Then, I fit the sides, front, and bottom. Next, I begin assembling the drawer.

To do so, place the front and sides in position on the bottom. Feel if the drawer front needs to be reduced in length so the sides are flush to the bottom. If you need to trim the drawer front, trim the back by the same amount.

Glue and nail the sides to the front. Then, glue and nail the back to the sides. Finally, glue and nail the bottom to the drawer. Fit each drawer to its opening, numbering the drawer and its opening as you go.

**Insurance.** When I have to do something 14 times, you can bet I'm going to make a jig to ensure my mind doesn't wander and cause me to make a fatal error at this stage of the project. This simple jig locates the holes for the bin pulls in the correct place. For the taller drawers on the bottom, I set the jig ³⁄₈" lower on the drawer front.

## HARDWARE AND FINISH

As on the original, I used bin pulls for the larger drawers and knobs for the smaller drawers in the center. To ensure I got the bin pulls located correctly, I made a quick drilling jig that I clamped to each drawer front. The jig ensured I didn't make a layout error.

The knobs are located dead center in the fronts of the smaller drawers.

Were I to make changes to this cabinet, it would be with the hardware. While I like the bin pulls, it would be more helpful to have pulls like an old library card catalog; the card could tell you what type of fastener is inside the drawer.

To solve this problem, Roy simply wrote what is in each drawer on the bin pull. I think he did it with pencil—it's almost impossible to see on camera.

Another thought: Add 2" of depth to the cabinet and you can hang hammers, screwdrivers, and other accoutrements of fastening and unfastening on the inside of the door.

Install the hinges and knob on the door. I used a magnetic catch to hold the door shut. Because I'm the only person who works in my shop, there's no need for a lock.

I finished the nail cabinet with two coats of garnet shellac, sanding between the coats. The cabinet hangs on my shop wall with a French cleat made from ½"-thick material. ■

## CUT LIST & MATERIALS

| | NO. | ITEM | DIMENSIONS (INCHES) | | | MATERIAL |
|---|---|---|---|---|---|---|
| | | | T | W | L | |
| ☐ | 2 | Sides | ½ | 10 ⅛ | 24 ½ | Pine |
| ☐ | 2 | Top/bottom | ¾ | 10 ⅛ | 17 ¼ | Pine |
| ☐ | 1 | Back | ⅜ | 17 ¼ | 24 ½ | Pine |
| ☐ | 2 | Door rails | ½ | 1 ⅞ | 17 ¼ | Pine |
| ☐ | 2 | Door stiles | ½ | 1 ⅞ | 24 ½ | Pine |
| ☐ | 1 | Door panel | ⅜ | 13 ¾ | 21 ⅛ | Pine |
| ☐ | 2 | Top frame stiles | ¾ | 2 | 18 ¾ | Pine |
| ☐ | 2 | Top frame rails | ¾ | 2 | 7 | Pine |
| ☐ | 4 | Side frame stiles | ¾ | 2 ¼ | 24 ½ | Pine |
| ☐ | 4 | Side frame rails | ¾ | 1 ¾ | 6 ½ | Pine |
| ☐ | 1 | Bottom frame front stile | ¾ | 2 | 19 ¾ | Pine |
| ☐ | 1 | Bottom frame rear stile | ¾ | 2 | 18 ¾ | Pine |
| ☐ | 2 | Bottom frame rails | ¾ | 2 | 7 | Pine |
| ☐ | 2 | Vertical dividers | ⅜ | 6 | 23 | Pine |
| ☐ | 6 | Horizontal dividers | ⅜ | 6 | 16 ¼ | Pine |
| ☐ | 12 | Wide drawer fronts | ¾ | 2 ½ | 5 ⅜ | Pine |
| ☐ | 12 | Wide drawer backs | ¼ | 2 ½ | 5 ⅜ | Pine |
| ☐ | 12 | Wide drawer bottoms | ¼ | 5 ⅞ | 8 ½ | Pine |
| ☐ | 6 | Narrow drawer fronts | ¾ | 2 ½ | 3 ¼ | Pine |
| ☐ | 6 | Narrow drawer backs | ¼ | 2 ½ | 3 ¼ | Pine |
| ☐ | 6 | Narrow drawer bottoms | ¼ | 3 ¾ | 8 ½ | Pine |
| ☐ | 36 | Top drawer sides | ¼ | 2 ½ | 8 ½ | Pine |
| ☐ | 2 | Wide lower drawer fronts | ¾ | 4 | 5 ⅜ | Pine |
| ☐ | 2 | Wide lower drawer backs | ¼ | 4 | 5 ⅜ | Pine |
| ☐ | 2 | Wide lower drawer bottoms | ¼ | 6 ⅜ | 8 ½ | Pine |
| ☐ | 1 | Narrow lower drawer front | ¾ | 4 | 3 ¼ | Pine |
| ☐ | 1 | Narrow lower drawer back | ¼ | 4 | 3 ¼ | Pine |
| ☐ | 1 | Narrow lower drawer bottoms | ¼ | 3 ¾ | 8 ½ | Pine |
| ☐ | 6 | Lower drawer sides | ¼ | 4 | 8 ½ | Pine |
| ☐ | 1 | Knob | | 17 mm | 15 mm | Antique brass |
| ☐ | 2 | Fixed-butt pin hinges | | 1 ¼ | 2 | Brass |
| ☐ | 7 | Flat knobs | | 1 ¼ | 1 | Antique brass |
| ☐ | 14 | Shell pulls | 3 ⅛ | | | Antique brass |
| ☐ | 1 | Magnetic catch | | | | |

# HANDPLANE CABINET

## Hard-working tools deserve a decive to rest.

**Hard-working tools deserve a decent place to rest.**

BY CHRISTOPHER SCHWARZ

O n certain holidays, such as New Year's Day, craftsmen in Japan clean their tools, put them on a shrine, and offer them gifts such as sake and rice cakes. It is their way of thanking the tools for the service they have provided and will provide in future days.

As my own collection of hand planes grew from a few rusty specimens handed down from my great-grandfather to a small arsenal of new high-quality instruments, this Japanese tradition began to weigh heavily on my mind. My planes generally squatted on my work-bench when not in use, and I had to constantly move them around to avoid knocking them to the floor as I worked.

After some thought, I decided that a cabinet dedicated to my planes was the best way to protect them from dings and to thank them for the ser-vice they provide almost every day of the year.

This piece is designed to be used either as a traditional tool chest that sits on a bench or as a cabinet that hangs on the wall on a tough French cleat. Because planes are heavy tools, the case is joined using

through-dovetails. The lid is a flat-panel door assembled using mor-tise-and-tenon construction. And the dividers inside the cabinet are screwed together so the configura-tion can be rearranged easily as my collection (or needs) change.

As you design your own version of this cabinet, you should measure your planes to ensure there's enough space for everything you own, or plan to own. This cabinet should provide plenty of room for all but the largest collections.

**DOVETAILS WITH THE PINS FIRST**

Because of all the cast iron and steel in hand planes, the cabinet's carcase needs to be as stout as possible to resist the stress that all this weight will put on the corners. In my opinion, the through-dovetail is the only joint for this job.

Whether you choose to cut pins or tails first (or use a dovetail jig and a router) is up to you. Usually I cut the tails first, but I try to keep an open mind about different techniques. So for a year I built as many things as I could by cutting the pins first—this is one of those projects.

Lay out the joints using the illustration at left, a marking gauge, a square, and a sliding bevel square set for 7°. I strike the lines with a marking knife and color them in a bit with a mechanical pencil. The pencil marks help me see the line and the knife lines keep me accurate. In fact, once you get some practice sawing, you should be able to easily remove the pencil marks from only one side of your knife lines. It sounds crazy, but it's actually not that hard.

There are many ways to remove the waste from between your saw's kerf lines. Some just chop it away directly with a chisel and a sharp

**DOVETAIL LAYOUT**

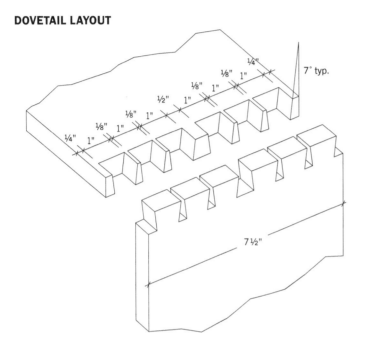

Mark the length of your pins and tails. There's a debate as to whether you should mark exactly how long you want them, a little less, or a little more. I prefer to mark them 1/32" longer so the ends are proud when assembled. Then I plane them flush after gluing.

Make the first cuts. Once the cut is started, hold the saw like you would hold a small bird that you're trying to prevent from flying away. Don't clench the handle; just keep enough pressure to avoid losing control. And never apply much downward pressure as you saw—this will cause your blade to drift.

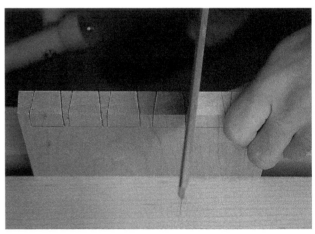

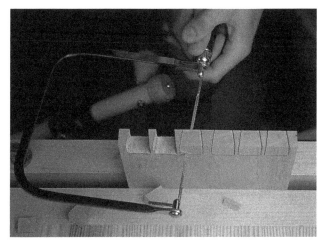

**Start to remove waste.** With the pins defined, get out a coping saw with a fine-tooth blade and remove as much waste as you can. The closer you get to the scribed line at the bottom of the joint, the less cleanup you'll have. But if you overshoot your line, you're cooked.

**Chisel time.** Clamp your pin board to a piece of scrap and remove the rest of the waste using a sharp chisel and a mallet. I sneak up on the line on one side, then on the other, then clean up any junk in the middle. Clean out the corners of the pins using a sharp knife.

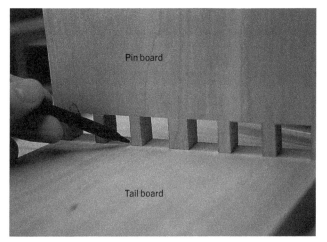

Pin board

Tail board

**Mark the tails.** Put your tail board on the bench with its inside face pointing up. Position its mate on top of it and mark the locations of the tails using a knife, followed by a mechanical pencil. Be careful not to shift either board during this step. If you do, erase your lines and start anew.

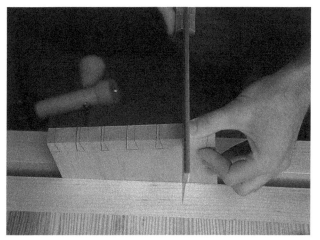

**Cut the tails.** Transfer the lines on your tail board across the end using a square. Clamp the board in a vise. I skewed the board in my vise so I'm actually cutting straight down. Angle the board one direction and make half of the tail cuts, then reverse the angle for the other cuts. Remember to cut ever-so-slightly outside of the lines.

blow from a mallet. I find that I'm sharpening my chisels less if I saw out most of the waste and chop out the little bit that's left. A coping saw with a fine-tooth blade works well, as does a jeweler's fret saw.

When you chop out the waste, be sure to stand so you can see the profile of your chisel—it must be perpen-dicular to the work. I use a standard bevel-edge chisel for this operation. Just make sure if you do the same that your chisel can be struck by a mallet without splitting the handle.

Next, you need to mark out the mating part of the joint by using the first half of the joint as a template. Here's the main difficulty you'll

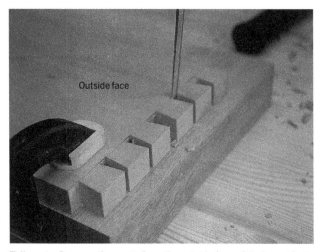

**Tail waste.** Remove the waste from the outside face of the board first, then remove the rest from the inside face. This will result in a neater joint if the grain buckles while you are chopping it. Again, clean up your corners with a knife.

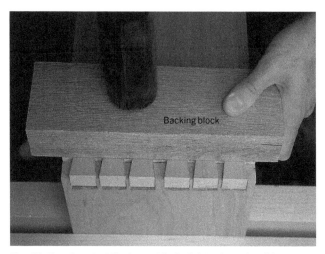

**Now it's time for a test fit.** Assemble the joint using a deadblow mallet and a backing block to distribute your blows across the entire joint. You should be able to push the mating pieces together most of the way using only hand pressure, plus a few taps to seat it in place.

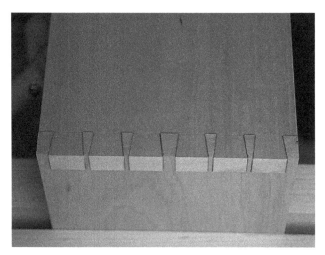

**Take a look.** You can see the pencil lines on the tails and how the ends of the pins and tails stick up a bit on the completed joint. This makes it easier to trim them flush, but more difficult to clamp during glue-up.

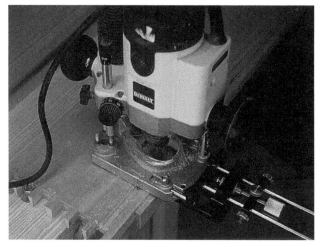

**Pin board groove.** The ½"-thick bottom sits in a groove cut in two passes using a plunge router outfitted with a straight bit and an edge guide. On the pin boards, you can cut the groove through the ends because it won't show.

encounter by cutting the pins first: You have to balance the pin board on edge to mark out the tail portion of the joint. With a small case, it's manageable. But with a dresser, it can be tricky.

Mark the joints with a sharp knife followed by a pencil. Then cut the tails. For this project I tried a tech-

nique you might want to take for a spin: As you can see from the photo at bottom right on p.149, I skewed the tail board in my vise so I was sawing straight down instead of at a 7° angle. I think this is a good trick for beginners as it makes it easier to track your lines. However, you have to shift the board 7° the other way for the other

## PLANES AT REST: ON THEIR SOLES OR ON THEIR SIDES?

One of the big debates among plane users is whether to place the tools on their soles or their sides when they are not in use. Traditional carpenters place the tools on their sides to protect the iron from getting dinged. Many woodworkers have picked up this tradition and it's frequently passed on from teacher to student (as it was to me).

But it might not be necessary.

A couple of years ago I was convinced by a fellow crafts-man that it's better to place planes on their soles when you are working at your bench. Here's the rationale. The old carpenter's rule applied to work on the job site, where you could never be certain about where you were setting your plane (this was back when you might actually see planes on a job site). So placing the plane on its side protected the iron from grit and gravel that could cover any flat surface in a newly built home. Also, carpenters say that putting planes on their sides prevents the iron from being pushed back into the plane's body, which is what could happen when a plane is rested on its sole.

Woodworkers, however, work on a wooden bench—far away from mortar dust and gravel. So they say it's best to place an unused plane on its sole to prevent the iron from getting dinged by another tool on the bench. What about the iron getting pushed up into the plane's body? If you think

about this statement for a moment, you'll see how ridiculous it is. The plane's iron is secured tightly enough in the plane's body to withstand enormous pressure as the plane is pushed through the work. It should be child's play for the iron to stay in one place with only the weight of the plane pushing it down.

Other woodworkers have come up with other solutions that work, too, including placing the planes sole-down over the tool well of their bench. Or they rest the sole on a thin wooden strip that holds the iron slightly above the bench. But I don't mess with that. After unlearning years of training, I now put my planes sole-down on the bench.

half of your cuts, so it's a bit more work.

At this point you have to pay close attention to your lines or your joint will have a sloppy fit. Saw on the waste side of the line, leaving the pencil line intact. This makes the joint just a little tight—something you can tweak by paring with a chisel.

Use a coping saw to remove most of the waste between the tails and chop the rest of the waste away with a chisel. Now you're ready for a dry run. Ease the inside edges of the tails just a bit with a knife. If the joint is too tight, try shaving off a bit on the inside faces of the pins—parts that won't show in the completed joint.

**Tail board groove.** On the tail boards, you need to stop the groove in one of the tails as shown. The dovetail layout shown in the illustration allows you to put the groove solidly into a tail.

**No dogs.** I don't like to clamp carcase pieces between dogs unless I have to—the clamp pressure can bow the pieces as I'm working them. I prefer a stop on my bench, as shown. After planing the case pieces, I'll hit them with some #220-grit sandpaper to remove any ridges left by the plane.

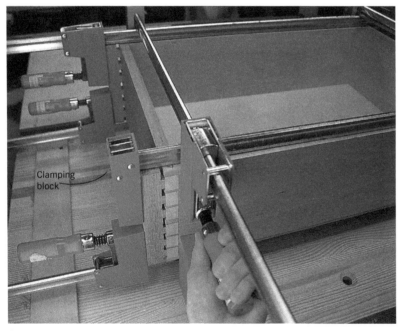

**Clamp them up.** I use simple clamping blocks to clamp the tail boards firmly against the pin boards. These are easy to make using a hand saw or band saw. Apply a consistent but thin layer of glue to the tails and knock the case together with the bottom in its groove. Clamp up the case using the clamping blocks and let it sit for at least 30 minutes.

## BOTTOM AND ASSEMBLY

Cut the remainder of your dovetails and mill the ¼"-deep x ½" groove for the plywood back/bottom. I milled this groove using a plunge router, a straight bit, and an edge guide. Make sure you put the groove ½" in from the bottom edge of the sides to make room for the French cleat that attaches the cabinet to the wall (if you're hanging this cabinet on a wall).

Before you assemble the case with glue, use a smoothing plane to prepare all the inside surfaces of the carcase for finishing—including the bottom piece. I sharpen a gentle camber on the cutting edge of the blade (about .002") and set the plane to take a very fine shaving, about .001" thick. This creates a surface that generally needs little or no sanding, especially with wood that has mild, easy-to-plane grain.

Once you glue up the case, trim the dovetail joints flush to the outside and use a smoothing plane to prepare the exterior of the case for finishing.

## BUILD THE DOOR

With the glue dry and the case complete, measure its width and length to determine exactly how big your door should be. You want the door to overhang the case by ¹⁄₁₆" on either end and ¹⁄₁₆" on the front, so size your door's rails and stiles accordingly.

As much as I enjoy handwork, I decided to cut the mortise-and-tenon joints for the frame-and-panel door using my "tailed apprentices" (my power tools). I begin making this classic housed joint by cutting a sample mortise with my mortising machine. Then, I cut all the tenons using a dado stack installed in my table saw.

**Door tenons.** A dado stack makes quick work of tenons for the door. The table saw's miter gauge guides the rails over the dado blades to cut the face and edge cheeks.

**Test the tenon in a test mortise.** When you're satisfied with the fit, cut the tenons on all the rails this way, being sure to check the fit after cutting each one.

**Mark the stiles.** Use the tenons to mark where the mortises should go on the stiles. I like this method because there is less measuring and therefore less room for error.

The rule of thumb is that your tenons' thickness should be one-half the thickness of your stock. The doors are ¾" thick, so the tenons are ⅜" thick with ³⁄₁₆" shoulders on the face cheeks.

Install a dado stack in your table saw. These tenons are 1" long, so I like to put in enough chippers to make a ⅝"-wide cut in one pass. Set the height of the dado stack to ³⁄₁₆" and set the fence so it's 1" away from the left-most tooth of your dado stack. Make several passes over the blade to remove the waste from the face cheeks, then remove the waste from the edge cheeks and test the fit in your sample mortise.

Raise the dado stack to ⅜" and remove the remainder of the waste on the edge cheeks. The bigger edge shoulders ensure that you won't blow out the ends of your mortises at glue-up.

Mark the location of your mortises using your tenons as a guide, as

## SLICK SOLE FOR SMOOTHING

When using a smoothing plane to prepare wood for finishing, you'll get better results if the plane's sole is waxed. The wax lubricates the sole and allows the plane to skim over the work. You'll use less effort and the end result looks better because you're less likely to stall during the cut. I use inexpensive canning wax, found at any grocery store, that costs a few dollars for a box. Apply the wax in the pattern shown here (keep it off the iron; that will change how the plane cuts). Then start working until you feel the plane becoming harder to move. Just reapply the wax and get back to work.

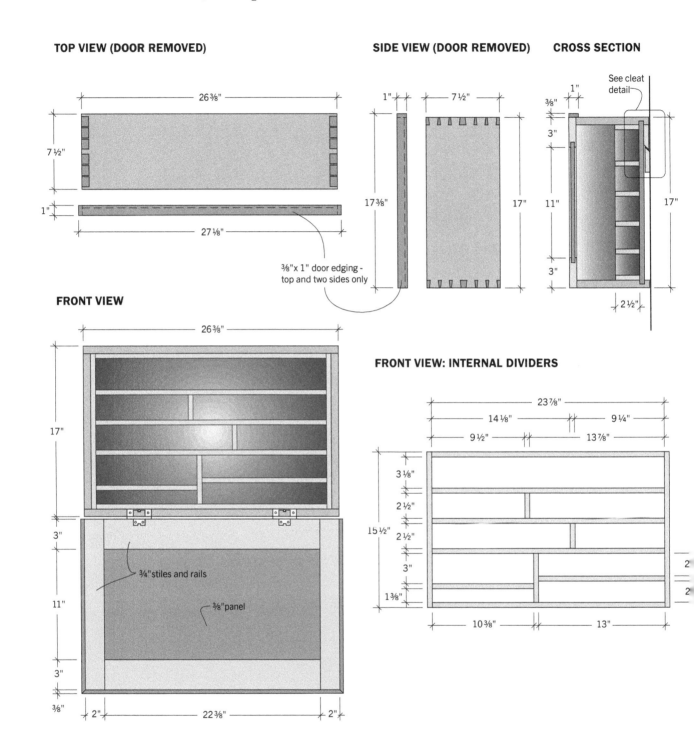

**TOP VIEW (DOOR REMOVED)**

26⅜"

7½"

1"

27⅛"

**SIDE VIEW (DOOR REMOVED)**

1"

7½"

17⅜"

17"

⅜"x 1" door edging -
top and two sides only

**CROSS SECTION**

See cleat
detail

1"

⅜"

3"

11"

3"

17"

2½"

**FRONT VIEW**

26⅜"

17"

3"

¾"stiles and rails

11"

⅜"panel

3"

⅜"

2"

22⅜"

2"

**FRONT VIEW: INTERNAL DIVIDERS**

23⅞"

14⅛"

9¼"

9½"

13⅞"

3⅛"

2½"

15½"

2½"

3"

1⅜"

10⅜"

13"

2

2

## CUT LIST & MATERIALS

| | NO. | ITEM | DIMENSIONS (INCHES) | | | MATERIAL | COMMENTS |
|---|---|---|---|---|---|---|---|
| | | | T | W | L | | |
| ☐ | 2 | Top/bottom | ¾ | 7 ½ | 26 ⅜ | Cherry | Cut ¹⁄₁₆" long. |
| ☐ | 2 | Sides | ¾ | 7 ½ | 17 | Cherry | Cut ¹⁄₁₆" long. |
| ☐ | 1 | Back | ½ | 16 | 25 ⅜ | Plywood | In ¼"-deep groove. |
| ☐ | 1 | French cleat for case | ½ | 2 ½ | 24 ⅞ | Maple | 45° bevel on one edge. |
| ☐ | 1 | French cleat for wall | ½ | 2 ½ | 22 ⅞ | Maple | 45° bevel on one edge. |
| ☐ | 5 | Divider top/bottom/long horizontals | ½ | 2 ½ | 23 ⅞ | Maple | |
| ☐ | 2 | Divider sides | ½ | 2 ½ | 15 ½ | Maple | |
| ☐ | 1 | Short horizontal divider | ½ | 2 ½ | 10 ⅜ | Maple | |
| ☐ | 1 | Mid horizontal divider | ½ | 2 ½ | 13 | Maple | |
| ☐ | 2 | Short vertical dividers | ½ | 2 ½ | 2 ½ | Maple | |
| ☐ | 1 | Mid vertical divider | ½ | 2 ½ | 4 ⅞ | Maple | |
| ☐ | 2 | Door rails | ¾ | 3 | 24 ⅜ | Cherry | Cut long to fit cabinet. |
| ☐ | 2 | Door stiles | ¾ | 2 | 17 | Cherry | Cut long to fit cabinet. |
| ☐ | 1 | Door panel | ⅜ | 12 | 23 ⅜ | Poplar | In ⅜" x ½" groove. |
| ☐ | | Door molding | ⅜ | 1 | 65 | Cherry | ¼" roundover on one edge. |
| ☐ | 2 | Forged flush rings, rectangle base | | 1 ½ | 2 | Brass | |
| ☐ | 2 | Colonial chest handles | | | | Brass | |
| ☐ | 2 | Non-mortise hinges | | ¾ | 2 ½ | | |
| ☐ | 2 | Magnetic catches | | | | | |

shown in the top right photo, page 153. Cut the ⅜"-wide x 1¹⁄₁₆"-deep mortises in the stiles using a hollow-chisel mortiser.

Next, cut the ⅜"-wide x ½"-deep groove on the door parts that will hold the panel. I use a rip blade in my table saw. Don't worry about stopping the groove in the stiles; the hole won't show on the front because it will be covered by molding. On the back you'll almost never see it because that is where the hinges go. If the hole offends you, by all means patch it with a scrap.

Assemble the door and make sure it fits on the case. When all is well, plane or sand the panel for the door

**Cut the mortise.** Cut one hole, skip a space, then cut the next one. Then come back and clean up the area in between. If you cut all your holes in a row, the mortiser's chisel can bend or snap because it wants to follow the path of least resistance.

**Install molding.** The ⅜" x 1" molding creates a dust seal around the edge of your cabinet and gives the piece a nice finished look. I cut a ¼" roundover on the inside edge of the molding. Miter the ends, then glue and nail the molding to the door's edges.

and glue up the door—making sure not to put glue in the panel's groove.

With the door complete, mill the molding that surrounds the door on three edges. Miter, glue, and nail it in place. Then install the hardware: butt hinges, catches, pulls, and handles.

## DIVIDE AND ORGANIZE

Finally, it's time to make the dividers for the planes. This is the easy part. I fastened the dividers using screws to make sure I could change the con-figuration in case my plane collection ever changed. The first step when building the dividers is to screw the four outermost pieces together and plane them down so they fit snugly inside the case.

Divide up the rest of your space and screw everything in place. Secure the assembled divider in the case with a couple of 1"-long screws. As this is shop furniture, I didn't choose a fancy finish. A few coats of clear lacquer is enough protection.

I hung my cabinet on the wall using a French cleat system, shown below. When installing the cleats, be sure to use 3"-long screws to fasten the cleat to the studs in the wall. This cabinet, when full, is quite weighty.

With this project complete and hung on my shop wall, I loaded the tools into their slots and thought for a moment about offering my planes some sake in the Japanese tradition. But then, coming to my senses, I offered myself a cold beer instead. ■

**Install the interior dividers.** It's a good idea to dou-ble-check your initial measurements against the real thing. I had a rude shock when my No. 4 plane was wider than I had anticipated. When everything looks good, screw all the parts together using #8 x 1" screws. Then screw the whole thing into the cabinet. I ran the screws in from the backside of the cabinet.

## THE GENIUS OF FRENCH CLEATS

When you hang a cabinet that will be loaded with heavy objects, I recommend a French cleat to fasten it to the wall. These cleats take a little more work than metal cabinet hangers, but they are well worth it because the cabinet will be more secure and it will be easy to put on the wall and remove.

To make a French cleat, take some of the ½" stock left over from building the dividers for the interior of your cabinet. You'll need one piece that's 24 ⅞" long, which you'll attach to the backside of the cabinet. And you'll need a second piece that's a couple of inches shorter than the first. Set your table saw to cut a 45° bevel and rip one long edge of each piece at 45°.

Glue and screw the long cleat to the top edge of the back-side of the cabinet with the bevel facing in. Now screw the sec-ond cleat to the wall where your cabinet will go—with the bevel facing the wall. Be sure to use big screws (I used #12 x 3") and anchor the screws in the studs in your wall.

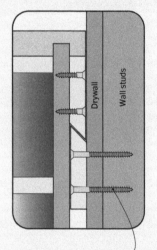

Drywall

Wall studs

Screws go through cleat and into studs.

# CABINET MAKER'S TOOL CHEST

## Store all the tools you need in easy reach.

BY ROBERT W. LANG

I f I were to make three lists—the tools I want, the tools I own, and the tools I need—the last would be the shortest. When I decided to build a wall cabinet for my hand tools, I put my most-used tools close at hand and at eye level, along with plenty of

drawer storage for tools I don't need so often.

I spent time sorting through my tools and experimenting. I cut some pieces of ¼"-thick foam core (plywood or cardboard would work as well) to pin down the size and shape

**Function first.** Plan the cabinet around groups of tools; put the most-often used ones where they will be near at hand.

**Rapid removal.** A trim router with a straight bit makes quick work of clearing waste between the pins, and it leaves a flat baseline.

**Plan meets reality.** With the case dry-fit, dados for interior partitions are laid out from a story stick.

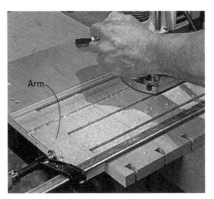

**Right angle.** This T-square jig indexes off the router cut in the arm. Line up that cut to your layout lines, then rout the workpiece.

of the cabinet and the layout of the tools. My goal was to store as much as possible in a compact and organized space.

### TAILOR THE PLAN

If you're thinking of building a tool chest similar to this, I suggest that you alter my design and adapt it to your tools, your shop, and the way you work. The results will be more useful to you, and you'll be happier.

I let function lead the way, with a single door for hanging storage. The stiles were turned 90° to provide

depth. I wanted to hang a framing square in a corner of the door, and a bit of experimentation led to an overall height of 30" and a width of 22 1/4". A survey of the tools destined to hang in the door led to an overall depth of the door at 2 1/2" and I settled on a case depth of 11 3/4".

My initial thought was drawers at the bottom of the case with hanging and shelf storage above. I didn't want the drawers too tall and I settled on varying heights from 1 1/2" to 2 3/8" with one taller narrow drawer. A mock-up of the plane ramp left room at the top and rather than redo my layout, I sketched in three 2"-high drawers at the top.

I thought that looked pretty good, found a few people to agree with me, and carried the horizontal division of the drawers down to the lower drawers. I wanted some wider drawers, and made those two-thirds of the space. Alternating the arrangement from side to side kept things interesting and the regular division meant fewer sizes to deal with.

### FROM THE OUTSIDE IN

The outer case is solid wood, connected with through-dovetails, as is the door frame. I laid out the dovetails to leave a half-tail where the case and door meet and half-pins at the wall and the outer edges of the door.

After sawing the pins by hand, I lowered the end of the board in my vise to place it even with the top of a piece of scrap on top of a box. Then I used a trim router with a straight bit to remove the waste between the pins, stopping short of the saw cuts. The small amount of material that

## EXPLODED VIEW

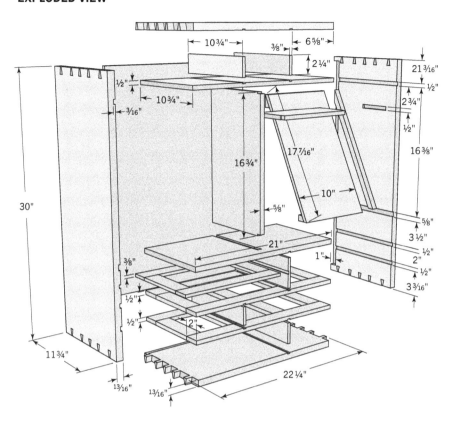

## FRONT VIEW

## CROSS SECTION

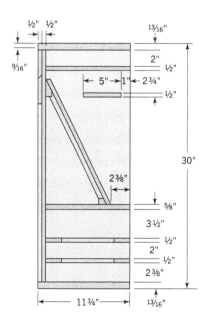

remained was cleaned out with a chisel.

With the pins complete, I marked and cut the tails then made the first of many trial assemblies. With a complex case like this, I lay out the joinery from existing parts when I can. With the outer case together, I marked the locations of the dados that capture the shelves and web frames.

I used a router with a straight bit and a right-angle guide to rout the dados. Because the dados are different widths, I set up a few different routers so I wouldn't need to change or repeat my tool setups. There are times when you really do need four routers.

There is a solid shelf below the top drawers and another solid shelf above the lower drawers. The two shelves are connected with a solid vertical divider that sits back 1" from the front edge. The dados for the vertical divider stop back from the front by 1½", and the front of the divider is notched at each end to cover the ends of the dados. After fitting the two shelves and the vertical divider, I reassembled the case, then cut and fit the front rails of the web frames.

Next, I laid out and cut the dados for all the vertical dividers between the drawers. These dividers have a short piece at the front glued cross-grain to a longer piece that runs front to back. These pieces are trapped in dados and have nowhere to go, even if the cross-grain joint should some-day fail.

The last set of dados are for the small shelf that sits above the plane ramp. These stop about ½" from the front edge of the shelf, which is notched beyond the ends of the dados.

With all the visible pieces in place, I made the secondary parts to complete the web frames. I made the back rails the same length as the fronts, and ran a groove down all the inside edges. I then cut stub tenons on the ends of the pieces that connect the rails front to back.

The web frames are glued together and dry fit to the case to make sure all parts fit tight and square. This dress rehearsal also showed where I needed to clamp during the final assembly.

**Fronts first.** Dados for the vertical dividers are also laid out with the carcase together, before the web frames that support the drawers are assembled.

**Take care.** Good openings will ensure good-fitting drawers. Check and adjust each opening with a dry assembly.

**Mark together.** Assemble the frame of the door before laying out the groove locations for the panels.

**Stop right there.** It's easiest to make stopped grooves by bringing the tool to the work. Plunge first close to the ends, then make the cut in between. A mortise chisel makes short work of squaring the ends of the grooves.

Then the case came back apart to clean up all the visible surfaces.

The back of the case is a piece of ½"-thick plywood that sits in ½"-deep rabbets in the sides. I skipped the rabbets in the top and bottom to avoid cutting into the dovetails at the corners. There is plenty of material in the area to screw the back to, and the top and bottom of the back are hidden behind drawers.

I clamped a straightedge to my layout line at the back of the sides and cut the rabbets with a large straight bit. A bearing above the cutter rode along the straightedge. I stopped short at the beginning and end of the cut and cleaned up the corners with a chisel.

## NOT YOUR AVERAGE DOOR

I made the door before I glued the carcase together, just in case I needed to adjust one or the other to ensure they fit together nicely. The outer corners of the door are simple through-dovetails. The extra stile in the middle of the door makes it a beefier structure and allows for two solid-wood panels.

A single dovetail at each end of the central stile holds it to the rails. This tail is lapped back to the edge of the groove that holds the panels, about 1" from the front edge. I dry fit the five frame parts, then marked the location of the groove with these pieces together.

The panels are ¾" thick, with a cove cut from both sides to leave a ¼"-wide tongue. The cove is a ½" radius and I set the front by eye until the cut looked pleasant, then lowered the cutter to make a smaller cut at the back. I then put a ¼"-diameter

## CUT LIST & MATERIALS

| | NO. | ITEM | DIMENSIONS (INCHES) | | | MATERIAL |
|---|---|---|---|---|---|---|
| | | | T | W | L | |
| ☐ | 2 | Case sides | 13/16 | 11¾ | 30 | Maple |
| ☐ | 2 | Case top/bottom | 13/16 | 11¾ | 22¼ | Maple |
| ☐ | 1 | Shelf above drawers | 5/8 | 10¾ | 21 | Maple |
| ☐ | 1 | Vertical divider | 5/8 | 9¾ | 16¾ | Maple |
| ☐ | 1 | Shelf below drawers | ½ | 10¾ | 21 | Maple |
| ☐ | 1 | Block plane shelf | ½ | 5 | 10⅜ | Maple |
| ☐ | 2 | Low web frame fronts | ½ | 2 | 21 | Maple |
| ☐ | 1 | Mid web frame front | ⅜ | 2 | 13⅞ | Maple |
| ☐ | 3 | 2" drawer dividers | ⅜ | 2¼ | 10¾* | Maple |
| ☐ | 1 | 2⅜" drawer divider | ⅜ | 2⅝ | 10¾* | Maple |
| ☐ | 1 | 3½" drawer divider | ⅜ | 3¾ | 10¾* | Maple |
| ☐ | 1 | Plane ramp | ½ | 10 | 17⁷/₁₆ | Baltic birch ply |
| ☐ | 2 | Plane ramp cleats | ¾ | ¾ | 10 | Poplar |
| ☐ | 1 | Case back | ½ | 21⅝ | 28⅜ | Baltic birch ply |
| ☐ | 2 | Low web frame backs | ½ | 2 | 21 | Poplar |
| ☐ | 8 | Web frame rails | ½ | 2 | 7¾ | Poplar |
| ☐ | 1 | Mid web frame back | ⅜ | 2 | 13⅞ | Poplar |
| ☐ | 2 | Mid web frame rails | ⅜ | 2 | 7¾ | Poplar |
| ☐ | 2 | French cleats | ½ | 4½ | 21⅝ | Baltic birch ply |
| ☐ | 2 | Door outer stiles | 13/16 | 2½ | 30 | Maple |
| ☐ | 2 | Door rails | 13/16 | 2½ | 22¼ | Maple |
| ☐ | 1 | Door middle stile | 1⅜ | 1⅜ | 30 | Maple |
| ☐ | 2 | Door panels | ¾ | 10³/₁₆ | 28⅞ | Maple |
| ☐ | 4 | 2" narrow drawer fronts† | 13/16 | 2 | 6⅝ | Walnut |
| ☐ | 1 | 2" long drawer front† | 13/16 | 2 | 13⅝ | Walnut |
| ☐ | 1 | 1½" drawer front† | 13/16 | 1½ | 13⅝ | Walnut |
| ☐ | 1 | 1⅝" drawer front† | 13/16 | 1⅝ | 13⅝ | Walnut |
| ☐ | 1 | 2⅜" narrow drawer front† | 13/16 | 2⅜ | 6⅝ | Walnut |
| ☐ | 1 | 2⅜" long drawer front† | 13/16 | 2⅜ | 13⅝ | Walnut |
| ☐ | 1 | 3½" drawer front† | 13/16 | 3½ | 6⅝ | Walnut |
| ☐ | 14 | Pulls | ⅜ | 11/16 | 1¾ | Maple |
| ☐ | 3 | Fixed-pin butt hinges | | 1 11/16 | 3 | Brass |
| ☐ | 1 | Full-mortise piano lock | | | | |

* Drawer dividers have a short piece at the front glued crossgrain to a longer piece that runs front to back. † Drawer backs and sides ⅜" thick. Back widths 5/16" less than sides; lengths same as fronts. Sides 10⁷/₁₆" long, same width as fronts. Bottoms ¼"-thick plywood; width 5/16" less than fronts; lengths same as sides. Create inserts to hang tools as desired.

**In sequence.**
There is a logical sequence to the final carcase assembly; with this many parts, it is worth a couple of practice runs to make sure everything fits.

**Square and tight.**
Liquid hide glue has a longer open time than yellow or white glue. That gives me time to make sure the corners are square and the joints are tight.

spiral-upcut bit in a small plunge router and cut the grooves in my door frames.

The door is sturdy and easy to put together as long as the panels can slide easily in the grooves. The center stile is fit to the top and bottom rails, the panels are slid into place, then the stiles go on either end.

### MOMENT OF TRUTH

If all of the carcase pieces have successfully gone together in the dry fit, final assembly can be done in one go. I made a couple of practice runs to be

sure of the sequence and that I had the right number and type of clamps ready.

I laid one side down on my bench, with the dados facing up. I brushed liquid hide glue (for its long open time) into the dados and on the end-grain surfaces of the dovetails. (Letting the glue wick into the end grain gives much better glue joints.)

Assembly is from the center out. I fit the large vertical divider into the two solid shelves, then placed the shelves into their dados. The small shelf above the planes also goes in at this time. Then, I placed the web frames, along with the small vertical dividers. There should be enough play between the frames and the shelves so that the dividers can drop into their dados.

Sliding the dividers in from the front would be silly unless the fit were too loose. If the fit is right they will get stuck before they get halfway back. With the dividers and frames all in place, I brushed more glue on the dovetails and added the top and bottom.

Before adding the second side, I brushed glue on the joining surfaces of the shelves and frames. Adding the second side is tricky, but not bad if the parts fit. I started the dovetails at the top and bottom, then lined up the shelves and frames and tapped them into the dados. When all the joints were started, I drove them home with a mallet.

If the dovetails fit, they shouldn't need to be clamped, but I needed clamps front and back at most of the dado joints. As I clamped, I checked to be sure that both the entire assembly and each corner was square. The final

**EXPLODED VIEW: DOOR**

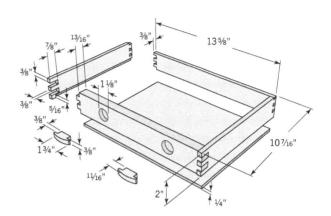

**EXPLODED VIEW: DRAWER**

step was to cut and fit the plane ramp from ½"-thick plywood. It attaches to ¾" x ¾" cleats nailed to the side of the case and the vertical divider.

## A FITTING STRATEGY

I have two methods to ensure nice-fitting drawers. The first is to fuss over the openings and try to get them as perfect as possible. The second is to fit the parts of the drawers to the openings before assembling the drawer boxes.

I start with the drawer fronts. After marking a rough layout with chalk, I cut the fronts slightly larger than the openings. I carefully trim each front until it just fits in the opening. I want a slight gap when I'm done, but at this point I aim for a snug fit.

I fit each side to easily slide into an opening. If there are any variations in the openings, I plane the edges of the drawer sides to compensate. My goal is a gap of ¹⁄₃₂" at the top of the sides. This means the sides can vary, so I mark each one with its location.

My theory is this: If the fronts and sides fit nicely, the assembled drawer should fit with minimal fuss, as long as the joints between them are correct. I chose to use Greene & Greene–style finger joints, but the principle applies no matter how the pieces are joined.

I started by laying out the joints on the fronts. Each has a ⅜" x ⅜" notch at the top and bottom corner and except for the two short drawers and the tall drawer, there is a ⅜" x ⅜"

**Fit first.** I make sure that the drawer fronts fit in their respective openings before assembling the drawers.

**In this corner.** A stop block on the jig (attached to the table saw miter gauge) is used to make identical cuts on all corners of the drawer fronts.

**This to that.** Much like a dovetail joint, the finished fingers of the drawer fronts are used to mark the sides for the matching half of the finger joints.

**A little higher.** The same jig is used to cut the fingers in the drawer sides. The saw blade is raised to the thickness of the drawer fronts plus 1/16".

notch centered vertically. The tall drawer has notches that line up with the notches in the short drawers next to it.

I made a jig from two pieces of plywood and attached that to the miter gauge of the table saw. I used a Freud box-joint cutter set to make 3/8"-wide cuts and set the height of the blade to 3/8" above the flat part of my jig. I ran the jig over the blade, then set the pieces vertically, lining up the layout lines to the edge of the cut.

For the corner cuts, I clamped a stop block to the jig; for the interior cuts, I positioned the fronts by eye.

These pieces are rather small, so I recommend clamping the work to the jig.

When the notches were all cut in the fronts, I cut a shallow rabbet in the back face behind the pins to make them easy to register on the sides and marked the joint locations with a pencil. (I fudged the sides down from the fronts about 1/32" when marking the joints.) This leaves the desired gap at the bottom of the drawer front after assembly.

I raised the blade by the thickness of the drawer fronts plus 1/16" and cut the fingers at the table saw. These joints should fit easily together with hand pressure only. When I had two sides connected to a front, I tested the fit in the corresponding opening. The offset in the joints raises the front, so I planed the top edge of the drawer fronts to leave a slight gap.

I cut the drawer backs to length, matching the distance from side to side of the dry-fit sides and fronts. The drawer bottoms fit in 5/16"-deep rabbets to maximize space in the drawer, so the width of the backs is 5/16" less than the sides. The backs and sides join with through-dovetails.

After cutting the back joints, I dry fit each drawer and made sure it fit in its openings before cutting the rabbets at the router table. The rabbet should be as narrow as possible because the drawers slide on what remains beyond the rabbet. After routing, I cleaned up the corners with a chisel.

**GET A GRIP**
Rather than throw money at the drawer pulls, I decided to make my own. I played around with the concept of a shaped wood pull in a shal-

## THE TOOLS I NEED & WHERE THEY LIVE

Hand tools have much in common with the medical profession. When you look at a catalog, or a list of recommended tools in a magazine or online, you see many specialists along with a few tools that tend to most tasks. The problem is that without experience, you can't tell which specialized tools you need (or want), or if problems are the fault of you or the tool.

Having too many tools, too early on, causes more problems than it solves. One saw will get you started. When you learn how to control it, you'll be able to assess its shortcomings and make an informed decision about what might suit you better. It's the same with chisels and planes. Start with one tool, learn how to sharpen and set it up, then use it.

If your goal is to make attractive and useful things, either as a hobbyist or a professional, you need to be familiar with all your options, both hand and power. If you're new to woodworking and stick with it, you'll eventually have a lot of tools, but the secret is to understand what they do and how they do it. That takes experience.

I started with a few good tools and added to them as my experience saw the need and my budget allowed. The following are the tools that I consider essential; they suit my budget and the way I work. Don't blindly follow my list—think about what makes sense for you and where you want to go with woodworking.

In my tool chest, marking, measurement, and layout tools are the most visible for very good reason. Buying good tools for those tasks was the first investment I made. My combination squares, marking gauge, and calipers plot the path before work begins, and check it when it is done. What matters is that the parts are the right size and in the right place—not what tool made them. If I were starting out, the first tool I would get would be a quality combination square. I also rely on a pair of fractional dial calipers, a 6" precision rule, a marking gauge, and a sliding bevel. Don't skimp with your layout tools.

Chisels aren't just for dovetails; they trim little bits and pieces left over from machine work, reach into places power tools can't, scrape excess glue away, and perform dozens of other tasks. Inexpensive chisels will teach you how to grind and sharpen (you won't have to worry about ruining the good ones), and the jobs that these can't easily tackle will let you know what specialized chisels to buy when you need them.

Smacking things is more specialized than you might think. You need something metal to pound nails, and something softer to beat on things a metal hammer would damage. A claw hammer and a dead-blow mallet are essentials, although I can justify the others in the photo and the other half-dozen I have tucked away.

Many woodworkers get by without a handsaw, but there are times when pieces are too small, too close to something else, or inconveniently located to cut by machine. Or the machine is set up for something else and a single cut needs to be made. One middle-of-the-road saw (in quality and price) will suit your needs, and may lead you to discover the situations where cutting by hand is more efficient, gives better results, or both. Practice with a single tool teaches you more than wondering which of the bunch to pick up.

I have more than a few handplanes, and they are called into service to refine the grunt work done by machines. My smoother removes machine marks faster and better than a belt sander or random-orbit sander, and my shoulder and rabbet planes tweak and refine joints that my table saw and router get pretty close. I began with a block plane, and it is still the plane I use most often. It is versatile and simple to set up and use, and its limitations taught me which of its more specialized brethren to add. Of course, if you are building a collection, you'll want one of each. If you're building furniture, experience will lead you to the tool kit that is best for you.

low hole. After settling on a design that looked and felt good, I needed to come up with a way to efficiently and safely make 14 pulls. I prepared a few pieces of maple ⅜" thick x ¹¹⁄₁₆" wide.

I laid out the pulls on the blank stock, leaving a couple of inches extra on each end. I set up at the drill press to hold the blanks at an angle below a 1⅛"-diameter Forstner bit, then lowered the bit to scoop the center of both sides of each pull.

I took the blanks to the table saw (where the ⅜"-wide box-joint cutter setup was still in place) and cut notches at the end of each pull. At the

**Make the target.** The face of the drawer front is marked directly on the fingers of the drawer side in the dry-assembled drawer.

**Hit the target.** The edges are rounded over to the pencil line with a file. The file also cleans up the saw marks of the end grain.

**Here's the scoop.** This blank will become a half-dozen pulls. After laying them all out, the Forstner bit makes an angled cut on each side to make a finger-friendly pull.

**The finished product.** The rounded-over fingers on the face and the ergonomically angled pulls make for handsome drawers.

band saw I cut the arcs on the other edge of the blanks, then separated the pulls. I refined the edges of the scoops with a gouge, rounded off the curved surfaces, then drilled a ³⁄₈"-deep x 1⅛"-diameter hole in the center of the narrow drawer fronts. The holes in the wide drawer fronts line up with the holes in the short ones.

With the drawer fronts and sides dry fit together, I marked the location of the drawer fronts on the fingers of the sides. I pulled the sides off and

rounded the edges of the fingers back to the pencil lines with a plastic laminate file. After that, I glued the drawers together, cleaned them up, and made sure they still fit.

**A HAPPY HOME**

I arranged the tools on the door in logical groups. My framing square is in the upper-left corner with my combination squares nested within the legs. The holders for the small squares have a rabbet in the top edge. That leaves a ledge to keep the stocks in place, and a notch in the end holds the blades. The curved shapes reflect the shapes of the stocks of the squares.

To the right of my squares is a block to hold smaller tools. The front and back are ³⁄₈" thick, separated by ½" x ½" squares. At the far right, the end extends above the front and ends in a semi-circle. A screw in the top secures that end to the door stile. At the other end, a screw goes through the block and into the center door stile.

In the lower half of the door is a rack for chisels, placed high enough to clear the drawer pulls. That rack is 1¼" wide, with 1"-diameter holes drilled on 1½" centers. The centers of the holes are ³⁄₈" back from the edge. I made saw cuts to square the ends of the openings so chisels can be put in from the front. Two screws through the outside of the door hold the rack in place. Plugs cover all the screws.

I cut some thin pieces of walnut to the shape of the back of my planes, and fastened them to the face of the plane ramp. I put the smooth and jack planes as far up the ramp as I could to make room for smaller planes below.

On the left side of the case is an open area; saws and hammers fit on walnut holders at the sides and back, leaving room for small power tools or my mug.

## AND SWING IT

The door is heavy on its own, and the tools inside add even more weight. I decided to go with three 1$\frac{11}{16}$" x 3" brass butt hinges. I centered the middle hinge vertically, and centered the top and bottom hinges on the top shelf and lowest web frame.

I routed the gains for the hinges $\frac{1}{16}$" deep. The hinges were not swaged, so I used a chisel and cut the outer edges of the gains deeper to leave the smallest possible gap when the door is closed.

The lock is a full-mortise piano lock let into the door halfway up. It has two wings that extend past the strike when the key is turned.

I sprayed shellac for the finish. The first coat was amber to warm the color, followed by two coats of clear. After letting this cure over a weekend, I took the sheen off with an abrasive pad and applied a coat of paste wax.

The back is screwed in place and the cabinet hangs on a French cleat— two 4$\frac{1}{2}$" wide pieces of plywood with a 45° bevel on one long edge. The cabinet side of the cleat is screwed to the shelf below the top drawers and the vertical divider. The other part of the cleat is screwed to the wall studs.

I'm not the most organized person, but I like the tools I use the most hanging near my bench. If I can't find a tool I need, then turn around to find the cabinet empty, I know it is time to stop and clean up a bit. ■

**Open-ended.** Chisels are gripped by the shape of the holes, while the open faces allow them to be put in place easily.

**Reflection.** This holder for an adjustable square uses the shape of the tool for its overall form. The slot holds the square securely when the door opens and closes.

**In the gap.** The $\frac{1}{2}$" space between the front and back of this simple rack provides flexible storage for tools I might need in a hurry.

**Router base.** A scrap clamped inside the door keeps the router base from tipping and the fence defines the back edge of the hinge mortises.

# NOT-SO-ORDINARY ROUTER CABINET

## Great shop storage isn't always built using plywood.

BY GLEN D. HUEY

As I look around my shop, or most woodworking shops, I see cabinets built with plywood and screws. But there are other options. I decided to change things up and make a shop cabinet using hardwoods, and to use the project to experiment with a couple of different techniques.

I consider a router an essential woodworking tool. And because I have router bits and accessories stored in small boxes stuck in drawers and in toolboxes (and hanging in less-than-ideal locations), a cabinet for all things router seemed the perfect project.

### BUILD THE FRAME

The first order of business is to select and mill wood for the sides, top, shelves, and center divider. Cut the top and sides to size, but leave the shelves and center divider ½" over-wide and overlong.

Dovetails are perfect to join the cabinet sides to the top; the joint—tails in the sides—holds up extremely well under the stress of heavy use and weight.

The dovetails are hidden by an applied molding—and if I'm hiding the work, I don't wish to see any indi-

cation of the joinery. To pull off the disappearing act, cut ⅛"-deep rabbets on the inside face of the ends of the top. This reduces the apparent thickness of the top as seen from the ends, but doesn't give up any actual meat. Plus, the small shoulder helps hold the cabinet square during assembly.

**Think ahead.** A wide pin at the rear of the top provides a solid area into which the side rabbets terminate, without showing from the outside of the cabinet.

**A way to hide.** A small rabbet cut into the ends of the cabinet top easily allows the joinery to be covered with full-thickness moldings.

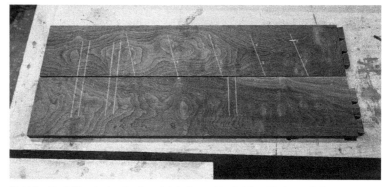

**Not identical.** The dados don't match in the cabinet sides. Work carefully as you mark the layout.

**Jig 1.** A simple square platform jig in conjunction with a bearing-guided router bit makes quick work of the straight dados.

**Jig 2.** A second simple jig—this one set at an angle, then reset in the opposite direction—knocks out the router-bit shelf dados.

**No stack needed.** Cut rabbets in two quick steps at the table saw—first with the stick flat the table, then on edge.

Position the sides on your bench with the insides up, rear edges touching. Mark the locations for all the shelves and the cabinet bottom. (All are ¾" thick, excepting the ⅝"-thick router bit shelves.) The tricky part is that the sides have different layouts. The left side has a 90° shelf and bottom and five router-bit shelves angled downward at 15°. The right-side layout is simply three ¾"-wide dados, laid out following the plan.

Now calculate and cut the center divider to width (leave it overlong) and the long shelf to length and width. The vertical divider nestles into ¼"-deep dados cut in the top and long shelf. Now's a great time to locate and mark the top and long shelf for those dados.

**ROUTER JIGS WORK BEST**

It's time to cut the ¼"-deep dados. I find two simple jigs are the best method of work. Each is built from scrap plywood and screwed together. The square platform jig is sized in thickness to work with a ¾" pattern bit. (My bit has a 1¼" cutting length, so if it's to cut a ¼"-deep dado, the jig has to be at least 1" thick.) Stack three pieces of ½" Baltic-birch ply, screw them together, then add a ½"-thick piece at one end to catch the workpiece and hold the jig square. (Fine-tune it as needed to bring the jig square to the workpiece.)

Align the jig to the left side of the cut and clamp it in position. A single clamp secures the jig. Rout the dado, allowing the bearing to ride against the jig. Stop your cuts about ½" from the front edge of the workpiece.

The angled dados are made the same way, except that the catch on

Lay out the pin board (the top) with a wide pin at the back. Make your saw cuts, remove the waste, then transfer the layout to the sides. Remember to set your marking gauge to match the remaining thickness on the top's end before scribing any lines. I use a band saw to define the tails, then clear away the waste with chisels and fit the dovetails. Because the joints are covered by molding, they don't need to be perfect.

When the joints slip together, you can see the value of the rabbets and how they help to hold the cabinet square.

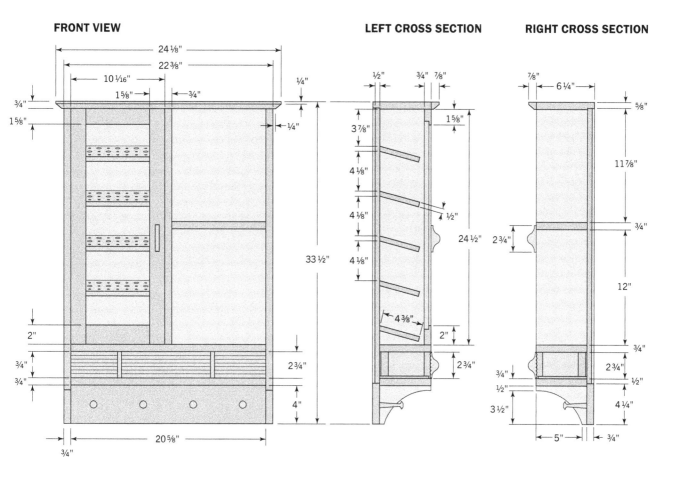

**FRONT VIEW**

**LEFT CROSS SECTION**

**RIGHT CROSS SECTION**

the bottom of the jig is angled to match the layout. The router bit I used here is ⅝" in diameter; I set it up in a second router for more efficient work. Cut the angled dados into the cabinet side so the top edge of the dado is 4½" long.

Before moving on, cut rabbets for the back and rear support (the peg board). I used a ¾" wide x 7/16"deep rabbet that I cut in two passes at the table-saw. I also cut a ¼"-deep rabbet along the back edge of the top to make sliding in the center divider easy. (This creates a slight gap at the sides, but it's covered by the molding.)

Next, align the divider to the left side, then transfer the layout of the bit shelves. Mark both the top and

**Exacting layout.** The best way to mark for the opposing-angled dados for the center divider is directly off the cabinet side.

**Step out.** Each of the parts housed in dados (except for the bit shelves) need to be notched at the ends; it's a simple and clean process using a table saw.

**Get level.** Small adjustments to get the angled shelves aligned makes it better to mark the single router shelf dado directly off the side location; measure, mark then rout.

**Odd arc.** With the limited height of the arc, it's best to slip a scrap into position to more easily use your compass.

**Your choice.** The top molding is attached to the cabinet to cover the dovetail joints. Use your favorite profile.

bottom of the dados to account for the jig's placement—always to the left of the cut. Before routing the dados, the angle of the jig needs to be reversed. Remove its catch, position the jig to the new layout lines, then locate and re-attach the catch in its new position. Rout the dados as before.

Now rout 90° dados into the top and the long shelf for the vertical divider. (See why I set up two routers?)

**PUZZLE COMES TOGETHER**

To fit the interior pieces of the cabinet, cut the shelves to length, then notch them to step out of the dados. I use a table saw for this. Set the fence for ¼" total cut (don't forget to account for the blade thickness), raise the blade to just more than ½", then, with a couple of quick passes, notch the ends.

Assemble the dovetail joints and slip the long shelf into position. With a couple of clamps holding things secure, fit the divider, making sure the angled dados align (small adjust-

ments are easily made). Notch the ends at the table saw, then slip the divider into position.

Next, mark the location of the router shelf on the divider. Measurements taken off the assembled cabinet better allow for level shelves. Cut the shelf to size and notch the ends before checking its fit. Repeat these steps to fit the bottom.

Now disassemble the cabinet and place the two sides inside up on your bench with the back edges matched. The last step is to lay out and cut the quarter-round design at the ends of the sides. The radius is 5"; the height is 3½". To facilitate using a compass for layout, slide a scrap along the bottom edge of the matched sides, then draw the half-circle (top center photo). Make the cut, then smooth the edges.

Sand the insides and assemble the cabinet. The two flat shelves, divider and bottom are fit in their dados and secured using screws and plugs. (It's simple, but this is a shop cabinet.) Glue and assemble the dovetails. Position the long shelf, then drill and countersink for the screws, two at each end. Repeat the steps for the divider and router shelf.

If you want to plug the divider holes in the long shelf, do that prior to attaching the bottom. There's little room to work after that shelf is installed. To wrap up assembly, fill the holes with plugs of matched grain, then after the glue dries, sand the surfaces smooth.

The cabinet is topped with a simple piece of molding cut with one of my favorite ogee bits, a classic design. Attach the molding using glue and pins. (Don't neglect to glue the miters.)

Now is the perfect time to add the rear support, which holds turned pegs. The support fits into the same rabbet you cut for the back. Two screws per end hold it in place. Lay out and drill for the pegs prior to installing the support.

## BUILD THE DOOR

Beginning woodworkers often build doors by joining the rails and stiles with mortise-and-tenon joints, then routing the back of the door using a rabbet bit. This results in a small section of exposed end grain at each corner. There is a better technique.

With just a couple of extra steps in the process, the rabbeted area is automatically formed in the assembled door. See "Build a Better Door" on page 174 for this method.

With the joinery on the rails and stiles complete, add glue to the joints, assemble the door in clamps, and allow the glue to dry. (After your finish is applied, install a clear acrylic panel, holding it in place with ¼"-square strips pinned in position.)

## DRAWER JOINERY

Because this drawer is meant to house small parts and accessories, the joinery does not require superhuman strength. I built it using a down-and-dirty method: a lock joint cut at the table saw (the key to accuracy is set-up).

Mill your drawer parts to thickness, width, and length. Install a dado stack in your table saw for a ¼"-wide cut, and set the blade height to ¼". Position the fence ¼" away from the stack, then cut dados at the ends of the drawer sides.

Now rabbet the ends of the back. I use a step-off block to align the stack with the ends of the front and back; a sacrificial fence is another option. Raise the blade height to ½", then rabbet the ¾"-thick drawer front.

With the blade height still at ½", switch over to a tenon jig to cut the tongues that lock into the dados. Position the jig and stack to cut dados leaving a ¼" of material at the inside face, as shown below.

When the cuts are complete and the parts fit properly, rabbet the bottom edge of the drawer front for the ¼"-thick drawer bottom. The bottom is pinned in place, but left overwide—

**Amazing hold.** For small drawers, a lock joint has incredible hold. While the short grain is brittle before assembly, when locked together, the joint is plenty strong.

## BUILD A BETTER DOOR

As we gain experience in woodworking, we find or learn new techniques that make our work better. A great technique to up your door-building game is to produce doors, which, with a few extra steps, have rabbets already in place for glass or flat panels. No more rabbeting after assembly.

Here's how it's done: Mill the rails and stiles to length, width, and thickness, then lay out and mark the mortises in your stiles; I chose ¼" shoulders for my tenons. Center the ¼"-wide x 1 ¼"-deep mortises in the stiles as you cut or chop the four mortises.

Now rabbet the inside edge of all four door parts. Cut ⅜"-wide rabbets as deep as the front wall of your mortises (½"). I prefer the table saw for this task, but there are other methods.

How the tenons are cut on the rails is where the huge difference in technique comes to light. Set the blade height to ¼" and set your fence to cut a 1 ¼" tenon. Don't forget to account for the ⅛" blade kerf. With the rail's front face against the tabletop, make a pass, cutting the rail.

Next, leave the blade height alone, but slide the fence to cut a ⅞" tenon (1 ¼"-⅜" rabbet). Make a pass cutting the rear face of your rails at all four locations. Before moving on, rotate the rail so the outside edge is facing the tabletop and make another cut. (There is no cut needed for the inside edge—it was removed by rabbeting.)

The difference in the procedure when making the cheek cuts is that you have two different blade heights with which to work: ⅞" for the back face and 1 ¼" for the front. Plus, you'll need to remove the shoulder waste using a band saw or handsaw.

As you slip the joint together, the extended shoulder at the back and outside edge of the rails fills the rabbeted area just as the front face snuggles tight to the stile. The rabbet for the glass or flat panel is done—and with no unsightly end-grain in sight.

**1. Rabbet.** After completing the mortises, rabbet the door parts flush with the front wall of the mortises.

**2. Tenons.** Set the fence to cut a 1 ¼" tenon with the blade set to just pierce into the rabbet.

**3. Back tenon.** Readjust the fence for a ⅞" tenon on the rail's back face.

**4. Cheeks.** Cut the cheeks using two different height adjustments—one for the front face and a second for the back.

**5. Fit together.** As the joinery slips together, the longer back tenons fills the rabbeted area just as the front tenon settles against the rail's edge.

you'll trim it to act as a drawer stop against the case back.

## DRAWER-FRONT DESIGN

A new approach for me was to texture the drawer front to add some visual interest with a series of grooves. I cut them with a ½" round-nose bit (also known as a core-box bit) at my router table, creating a series of small arcs in the front.

The secret (if there is one) is to start your layout, and the cuts, at the center of the drawer front and work toward the edges. Take the time to align the first cut down the centerline (it needs to be very close, but there is a bit of course correction possible from a second pass). After the first pass, reverse the front and make a second pass. This may widen your groove, but it will not be noticeable, and it guarantees you're centered. (As always, test pieces make setup easier.)

Slide your fence closer to the bit for the second and third grooves, making sure there is no flat between them. Repeat these steps for the fourth and fifth cuts (an odd number of grooves makes the layout much easier). With the drawer front textured, sand the grooves (a sandpaper-wrapped dowel works well), then glue up the drawer.

As the glue dried, I designed a few small pieces to use as pulls for the drawers and door. I began with ⁷⁄₁₆"-wide stock, then laid out a simple undulating pattern. I made the cuts at the band saw, smoothed the pieces at a spindle sander, and eased the edges using sandpaper.

The drawer pulls are set into dados cut in the drawer front. Determine

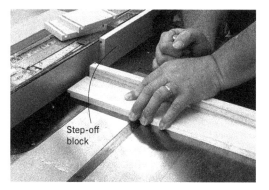

**Dado stack.** Here, I'm cutting a rabbet on the end of the drawer back. Note the step-off block to align the workpiece with the blade.

Step-off block

**Flush to the lip.** The last cut using the dado stack is to create the slot for the ends of the drawer sides. Position the cut at the top of the rabbet.

the location for the pulls (I used them to equally divide the two sections of the cabinet), then make marks along the edge of the drawer front to show the start and stop points of the dados.

Set your table saw blade to cut just below the deepest point of your decorative drawer grooves and align the blade with your layout marks. Using the miter gauge, nibble away at the cuts until you've achieved the thickness of your pulls—check this with each pass when you get close to the second layout line. Repeat the steps for the second pull, then glue the pulls in place.

Wrap up work on the drawer by pinning the drawer bottom to the completed drawer box.

## FIT AND FINISH

Fit the door to its opening, making any needed adjustments to its width

## CUT LIST & MATERIALS

| | NO. | ITEM | DIMENSIONS (INCHES) | | | MATERIAL | COMMENTS |
|---|---|---|---|---|---|---|---|
| | | | T | W | L | | |
| ☐ | 2 | Sides | 3/4 | 6 1/4 | 33 1/2 | Walnut | |
| ☐ | 1 | Top | 3/4 | 6 1/4 | 22 3/8 | Walnut | |
| ☐ | 1 | Bottom‡ | 3/4 | 5 1/2 | 21 3/8 | Walnut | |
| ☐ | 1 | Long shelf‡ | 3/4 | 5 1/2 | 21 3/8 | Walnut | |
| ☐ | 1 | Vertical divider‡ | 3/4 | 5 1/2 | 25 | Walnut | |
| ☐ | 1 | Router shelf‡ | 3/4 | 5 1/2 | 10 9/16 | Walnut | |
| ☐ | 5 | Bit shelves‡ | 5/8 | 4 7/8 | 10 9/16 | Walnut | One edge angle cut.* |
| ☐ | 1 | Rear support | 3/4 | 4 1/4 | 21 3/4 | Walnut | |
| ☐ | 1 | Back | 1/2 | 21 3/4 | 28 5/8 | Plywood | |
| ☐ | 2 | Door stiles | 3/4 | 1 5/8 | 24 1/2 | Cherry | |
| ☐ | 1 | Upper door rail | 3/4 | 1 5/8 | 9 5/16 | Cherry | 1 1/4" TBE† |
| ☐ | 1 | Lower door rail | 3/4 | 2 | 9 5/16 | Cherry | 1 1/4" TBE† |
| ☐ | 1 | Window | | | | Clear acrylic | Fit to rabbets. |
| ☐ | 1 | Backing strip | 1/4 | 1/4 | 56 1/2 | Cherry | Fit to rabbets. |
| ☐ | 1 | Drawer front | 3/4 | 2 3/4 | 20 5/8 | Cherry | |
| ☐ | 1 | Drawer back | 1/2 | 2 1/2 | 20 5/8 | Poplar | |
| ☐ | 2 | Drawer sides | 1/2 | 2 1/2 | 5 | Poplar | |
| ☐ | 1 | Drawer bottom | 1/4 | 5 1/2 | 20 7/8 | Poplar | |
| ☐ | 3 | Pulls | 7/16 | 2 3/4 | 1 | Walnut | |
| ☐ | 1 | Crown molding | 3/4 | 7/8 | 48 | Walnut | |
| ☐ | 4 | Pegs | | 1/2 | 3 1/2 | Walnut | |
| ☐ | 2 | Non-mortise hinges | | 11/16 | 2 | Bronze-coated steel | |
| ☐ | 2 | Rare-earth magnets | 1/8 | 1/2-dia. | | | |

* Front and back edges are ripped at a 15° angle. † Tenon both ends. ‡ These pieces are 1/2" overwide and overlong versus the measured drawing; cut to fit as indicated in instructions.

and height. I used simple no-mortise hinges and a shop-made catch with two rare-earth magnets—one on the triangular catch, one buried in the door (don't glue the magnets in place before checking their polarity). The door pull is simply glued in place.

Lay out and drill holes in the router-bit shelves to accept the shafts of your router bits (know that your layout needs may vary).

I needed storage for both 1/4"- and 1/2"-shank bits. I mixed up the layout so each shelf holds both sizes. A simple L-shaped jig and filler pieces cut to 1" width make the task easy; it has to be, because there are 27 holes in each shelf.

Make the L-shaped jig from scrap plywood. Position the point of a 1/2"-diameter Forstner bit at the middle of the shelf approximately 1" from the edge. Place four spacers next to the end of the shelf, then fit the jig against the first spacer and the shelf. Clamp the jig secure.

**Layout is key.** The first groove for the drawer-front texture should be perfectly centered in the face. (Or you can get darn close and make a second pass with the stock reversed.)

**Subsequent grooves.** Adjust the fence to make the next-in-line cuts in the texture pattern—working with grooves in odd numbers makes the layout work easier.

**Rather catchy.** A simple catch with a rare-earth magnet epoxied at the center is glued and pinned inside the door; another magnet is installed in the door.

Remove the spacers, slide the shelf tight to the jig to drill the first hole, closest to the right end of the shelf. Slip two spacers (equal to 2") between the jig and shelf to drill the second hole. Complete the five ½"-diameter holes by repeating these steps, then drill the holes in the remaining four shelves.

To drill the ¼"-diameter holes between the ½" holes while keeping the spacing at 1", switch drill bits and begin the process with a single spacer set between the jig and the shelf. As before, add two spacers with each hole as you work across the shelf. Complete the five shelves.

I used the same process to drill only ¼"-diameter holes along the front edge of the shelves, then realigned the jig to drill the center row of alternating diameters. If you pay attention as you work, it's an easy task to complete.

Before installing the shelves in the cabinet, plane or cut the rear edges at a 15° angle to match the slope of the shelves, then slip them into their dados. The cabinet back holds the angled shelves in place.

The back is plywood. Install it with screws after completing the finish.

Here, too, I, decided to switch things up a bit from my usual approach. Instead of shellac, I used a water-based topcoat. And to try it two ways, I brushed on the first coat, but sprayed the second after a thorough sanding with #320-grit. (I wasn't surprised to find that I preferred the sprayed coat.)

My first thought as I finished the cabinet was that, had I not angled the router-bit shelves, this piece could have found its way into my house. But with the bit shelves in place, I've built a nice shop cabinet from something other than plywood. Plus, I played with a couple of new techniques along the way. And I have a great cabinet to help get a handle on my router bits and accessories. ■

# ARTS & CRAFTS TOOL CABINET

## The goal: the maximum tools in the minimum space.

BY CHRISTOPHER SCHWARZ

Sometime while sawing the 60th dovetail for a drawer side, when my patience was as thin as the veneer facing on cheap ply-wood, a familiar feeling crept into my body. I began to experience an understandable lust for my biscuit joiner.

It sat patiently on a shelf, and I knew that its chattering, rattling teeth would make everything about this tool cabinet go much faster. But I resisted, because I had the words of a Victorian social reformer, art critic, and part-time madman ringing in my head.

The writings of Englishman John Ruskin (1819–1900) were a cornerstone of the American Arts & Crafts movement. Ruskin decried the worst parts of 19th century industrialism. He promoted craft, pensions, and public education when there were little of those things for the poor.

And in his book *The Seven Lamps of Architecture, The Lamp of Memory,* which was published in 1849, he wrote a passage that all woodworkers should read. It's a bit long and a bit dramatic, but it has stuck with me just the same.

"When we build, let us think that we build forever. Let it not be for present delight nor for present use alone. Let it be such work as our descendants will thank us for; and let us think, as we lay stone on stone, that a time is to come when those stones will be held sacred because our hands have touched them, and that men will say, as they look upon the labor and wrought substance on them, 'See! This our father did for us.'"

The biscuit joiner stayed on the shelf. I continued to saw, chop, pare, and fit for another four or five hours. Ruskin, I hope, would have approved.

### FROM THE BOOK OF TOLPIN

While Ruskin kept me going through this long and difficult project, I really have a 20th century craftsman and author to thank (or blame) for my obsession with building a fine tool cabinet. Since it was first published in 1995, *The Toolbox Book* by Jim Tolpin has become the most-thumbed book in my library. I've studied every page, toolbox, and drawing between its maroon cover boards (the dust jacket is long gone).

Years ago, I resolved to build myself a cabinet that might rival some of Tolpin's examples. For an entire year, I spent many spare moments doodling on graph paper and on my computer to come up

## SIX STORAGE SOLUTIONS

Tools need to be protected, organized, and easily retrieved. That's a tall order.

Here are some of the problems I've run into over the years: Hanging tools on a wall keeps them organized and close at hand, but unprotected. Keeping them in a traditional sliding tool till in a chest keeps them protected and organized, but you dig around for them endlessly. Drawers under a bench keep them protected and close at hand, but most drawers end up a jumbled mess.

Here's my solution, and so far it works well. The cubbyholes are sized exactly to hold a full complement of hand planes. Finding the right plane and getting it down for use has never been easier.

The chisel rack puts my most-used sizes out where I can get them. And the rack is designed to hold the tools even when the door is accidentally slammed.

The saw till on the right door is the same way. These two saws do 80 percent of my work and they're always handy.

The real feature is the drawers. The smaller drawers hold tools for a specific operation. In the larger drawers, the interchangeable trays stack inside the drawers and also hold tools for a specific operation. Whenever I dovetail, I grab the top right drawer. No more making mounds of tools on the bench.

**1. Chisel rack.** This simple L-shaped bracket holds the five chisels I use most, plus my drawbore pins. Don't use a magnetic strip; it will magnetize your tools, which makes them difficult to sharpen.

**2. Tool trays, lower drawer.** The bottom of the drawer is for the tools I rarely need. The tray at left holds files and rasps (I'm going to subdivide this tray as soon as some more rasps arrive in the mail). The tray at right holds specialty chisels and screwdrivers.

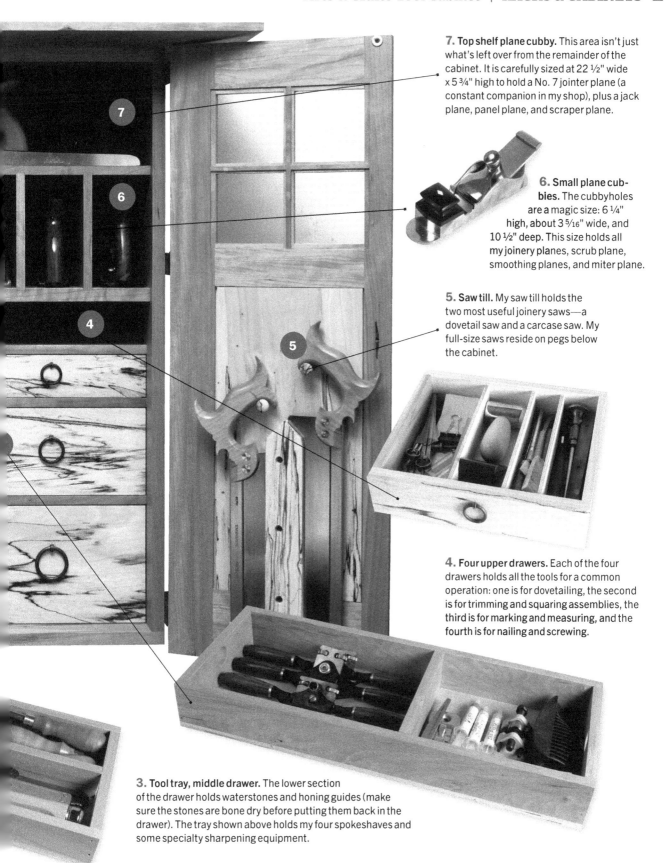

**7. Top shelf plane cubby.** This area isn't just what's left over from the remainder of the cabinet. It is carefully sized at 22 ½" wide x 5 ¾" high to hold a No. 7 jointer plane (a constant companion in my shop), plus a jack plane, panel plane, and scraper plane.

**6. Small plane cubbies.** The cubbyholes are a magic size: 6 ¼" high, about 3 5/16" wide, and 10 ½" deep. This size holds all my joinery planes, scrub plane, smoothing planes, and miter plane.

**5. Saw till.** My saw till holds the two most useful joinery saws—a dovetail saw and a carcase saw. My full-size saws reside on pegs below the cabinet.

**4. Four upper drawers.** Each of the four drawers holds all the tools for a common operation: one is for dovetailing, the second is for trimming and squaring assemblies, the third is for marking and measuring, and the fourth is for nailing and screwing.

**3. Tool tray, middle drawer.** The lower section of the drawer holds waterstones and honing guides (make sure the stones are bone dry before putting them back in the drawer). The tray shown above holds my four spokeshaves and some specialty sharpening equipment.

with a design that satisfied the three things I wanted from a cabinet: It had to hold a lot of tools, look good, and be built to last. After studying my work habits, measuring all my tools, and paging through thousands of examples of Arts & Crafts casework, this is what I came up with.

It's small but spacious. Have you ever ridden in an old Volkswagen Beetle? They are surprisingly roomy, and especially generous with the headroom. Somehow, the Beetle violates the laws of space and physics, and it is roomy but can also be parked between two oversized Hummers. This cabinet is designed to function the same way. The interior is a mere 11¼"- deep, 22 ½" wide, and 31½" tall. Yet, thanks to good planning, it holds every hand tool I need.

The cubbyholes and shelf for hand planes are carefully sized for all the planes needed in a modern shop. The drawers are loaded with trays of tools. Each tray contains all the tools for a routine function, such as dovetailing, sharpening, or shaping curved surfaces.

The cabinet looks pretty good. I spent months thumbing through old Art & Crafts furniture catalogs and contemporary hardware catalogs for inspiration. This cabinet and its lines are a little bit Gustav Stickley, a little Harvey Ellis, and a little of myself.

The cabinet will endure. No compromises were made in selecting the joints. Every major component (with the exception of the changeable, nailed-together trays) are built to withstand heavy use. Of course, when you discuss durable joints, you are usually talking dovetails, which is where we'll begin construction.

## A CASE THAT TAKES A BEATING

When this cabinet is fully loaded, my best guess is that it weighs more than any single member of our staff at *Popular Woodworking* (modesty prevents me from revealing what that upper limit might be). To ensure the bottom and top pieces can withstand this weight, I joined them to the side pieces with through-dovetails.

One interesting variation worth noting here is that instead of using one solid top piece, I substituted two 3"-wide rails and dovetailed them into the sides to save a little weight. Because I cut these dovetails by

**Sawing the tails.** Clamp the two sides together and cut them at the same time. This saves time and effort and prevents layout errors.

**Clean up the rabbets.** If your rabbets for the back are perfectly square, your case is much more likely to end up square, too. Clean up any imperfections with a rabbeting plane, such as this bullnose rabbet plane.

hand, it was simple to lay out this unusual arrangement. If you plan to use a dovetail jig, you will save yourself a headache by forgetting the rails and making your top one solid piece instead.

If you're cutting the dovetails by hand, it's faster and more accurate to clamp your two sides together and saw the tails on the side pieces simultaneously. For years I resisted this technique because it seemed more difficult, but now I know better.

A second feature of the case to note is that the rabbet for the back is a hefty 1" wide. This allows room for the ½"-thick shiplapped back, plus a ½"-thick French cleat that will park the cabinet on the wall and keep it there.

And then there are the stopped dados. These ¼"-deep joints in the side pieces hold all the dividers. Cutting these joints is simple work with three tools: a plunge router, a bearing-guided straight bit, and a shop-made T-square jig that guides the whole shebang. Lay out all the locations of your dados on the sides. Park the jig so it lines up with your layout lines. Cut the dados in two passes.

Fitting all the horizontal dividers to fit the dados is easy. The ½"-thick dividers simply need a small notch at the front to fit over the rounded end of the dado created by the round straight bit. A sharp backsaw is just the tool here.

The ¾"-thick horizontal divider needs a bit more work to fit in the ½"-wide dado. A ¼" x ¼" end-rabbet is the answer.

The through-dados that hold the vertical dividers use the same router jig, but with the plunge router set to make only an ⅛"-deep cut. Laying out

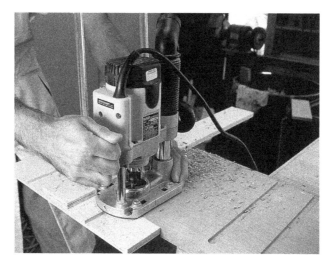

**Rout the dados.** The shop-made T-square jig and a plunge router make quick work of the dados.

**Jig setup.** Here you can see how you use the dado cut into the jig to line up the jig with your layout lines. Using a router with a flat side on its base is more accurate than using a router with a round base.

the locations of these parts for the hand plane cubbyholes might seem daunting. If you want the openings evenly spaced, they should each be 3.333" wide. I don't have any infinite numbers on my ruler. But it's actually child's play to lay out the cubbyholes with a pair of dividers (they look like a school compass but with two pointy tips—no pencil). You can tweak these tools until they step off the cubbyholes as precisely as you please. Dividers are one of my secret weapons.

With all these parts cut and fit, make the back of the case. I used

**Fit the dividers.**
This is easy with a handplane. I merely make sure the dividers are surfaced a few thousandths of an inch thicker than where I want them to be. Then I thin them down with a smoothing plane until they slide in with just a little persuasion.

**Flush the dovetails.**
After gluing the sides to the bottom and top rails, trim the dovetails flush with a block plane. Soak the end grain with a little bit of mineral spirits to make it easier to cut. Here you can also see how I supported the case as I worked on it. The big slab holding up the side is an offcut from an old door that's clamped to my bench.

ambrosia maple. It's cheap and looks a bit like the spalted maple I used in the doors and drawers. The back boards are joined by a ¼"-deep x ⅜"-wide shiplap on each long edge.

The top cap is easy. Cut the wide chamfer on the underside using your table saw. Clean up the cut with a block plane. Attach the top to the rails with screws.

You are now at a critical juncture. You can go ahead and get some quick gratification and assemble the whole case. But good luck when you go to finish it. Getting those cubbyholes finished right will be murder. The better solution is to glue up only the sides, bottom and top rails. Tape off the exposed joints and finish all the case parts (I used two coats of a satin spray lacquer). Then assemble the case. I know it sounds like a pain (it is). But the end result is worth it.

Finish the back pieces and top cap while you're at it. Now you can screw the back in place and the top cap. You are ready for the doors and drawers.

**EASIER THAN THEY LOOK**
The doors aren't too bad. The muntins that form the four lights in each door appear difficult, but thanks to a little sleight of hand, it's no problem.

But before getting mired in those details, you need to assemble the doors. Here's how they work: The stiles and rails are joined using mortise-and-tenon joints. For mid-size doors such as these, I use ⅜"-thick x 1"-long tenons.

Cut your tenons and your mortises, then mill a ¼"-wide x ⅜"-deep groove in the rails and stiles to hold the door panel. I generally make this groove on the router table using a straight bit and featherboards. It's the easiest way to make the groove start and stop in the right place in the stiles.

The door panel needs a rabbet on its back to fit in the groove. But before you mill the panel, you should know a bit about spalted maple. Its black spidery lines are caused by the spalt fungus, which attacks the tree after it's been felled. In short, it's partly rotted.

It's always best to wear a respirator when dealing with spalted wood. There are numerous accounts of people who have had respiratory problems after breathing in the dust.

Once you fit the panel, assemble the doors—the muntins are added after assembly. Once the glue cures, cut a ¼"-wide x ½"-deep rabbet on the backside of the opening for the glass. This rabbet will hold the narrow backing strips that are built up into the muntins. The photos at right explain it better than words can. Essentially, you create the T-shaped molding that makes the muntins by gluing together ¼"-thick x ½"-wide strips of wood. It's simple work.

What's not so simple is mounting the doors with the strap hinges. These hinges are inexpensive, beautiful, and handmade. As a result, they need a bit of tweaking and bending and hammering and cursing to get them just right to hang a door.

Here's my best tip: Screw the hinges in place with the cabinet on its back. Then stand it up, loosen the hinge screws and make your final adjustments. I used a block plane to make some adjustments, and a mallet for others. Let your frustration level be your guide.

**Rabbet.** Cut the window rabbet on the backside of the door using a rabbeting bit in your router table. With a large tabletop such as this, it's simple work.

**Apply glue.** Glue one backing strip into the rabbet in the door on edge. Then flip the door over and glue a vertical muntin onto the backing strip. Then use spring clamps to hold everything while the glue dries.

**More glue.** Install the horizontal muntins the same way. First, glue a backing strip into the rabbet on the backside of the door. Then flip the door over and glue the muntin to that.

**FRONT VIEW (DOORS CLOSED)**

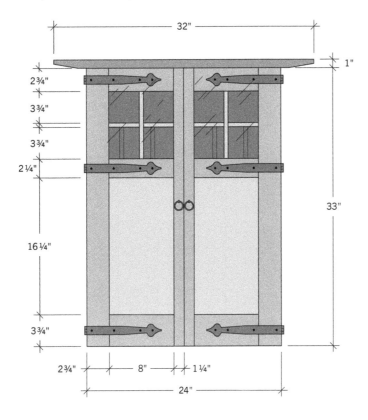

**SIDE VIEW**

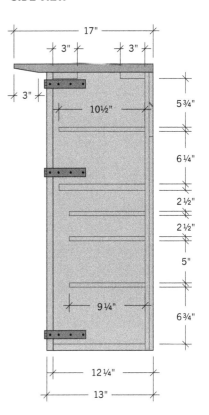

**FRONT VIEW (DOORS OPEN)**

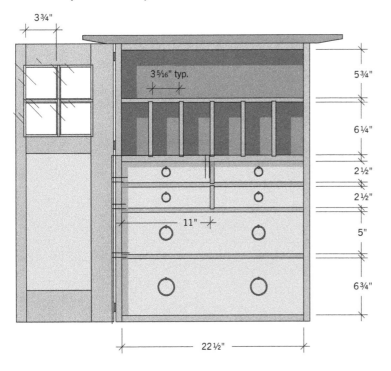

### GETTING A HANDLE ON DRAWERS

The drawers are a long slog. Even though I'm a fair dovetailer, it took me three solid days of work to get the drawers assembled and fit. But before you start listening to that lock-miter router bit whispering in your ear, remember this: The drawers are going to hold a tremendous amount of steel. And when you open the drawers during a future project, you'll never be disappointed to see dovetails.

To make things a tad easier, I built all the drawers using through-dovetails and ½"-thick material for the front, sides, and back. Then, with the drawer glued up, I glued on a ¼"-thick piece of spalted maple to the front piece. This trick also allowed me to stretch my supply of spalted maple.

The four small drawers are built a little differently than the two larger ones. Because the small drawers are shallow, I wanted to use every bit of space. So the bottom is ¼"-thick plywood that's nailed into a ¼" x ¼" rabbet on the drawer's underside.

The larger drawers are more conventional. Plow a ¼" x ¼" groove in the sides and front pieces to hold a ½"-thick bottom, which is rabbeted to fit in the groove.

Build all the drawers to fit their openings exactly, then use a jack plane to shave the sides until the drawer slides like a piston. Finish the doors and drawers, then it's time for the fun part: dividing up the drawers, building trays for the tools, and tweaking the hardware so everything works just right.

As you divide up the drawers and trays, one word of advice: Don't fasten any of the dividers permanently. Your tool set will change, and you want to be able to easily alter the dividers. I fit mine in place with friction and a couple 23-gauge headless pins. The dividers can be wrenched free when I need room for a new tool.

When you hang the cabinet, use wide cleats—mine were each 5" wide. This allows you to get more screws into the cabinet and studs. Also, for extra insurance, I rested the bottom of the cabinet on a 2"-wide ledger that also was screwed into the studs.

With the project complete, the voice of Ruskin was finally silenced for a short time as I assessed my work. (I for one was happy for the silence; Ruskin vacillated between madness and lucidity during the last years of his life.) I scolded myself for a few things: the reveals around the

**Assemble.** Build the drawers with through-dovetails. Then glue a piece of ¼"-thick veneer to the front.

**Install the bottoms.** There are two different ways of installing the drawer bottoms. The bottom in the top drawer rests in a rabbet in the sides. The drawer bottom for the larger drawers slides into a groove.

**Add drawer dividers.** Install them so they can be easily removed in the future. A 23-gauge pinner is an excellent tool for this job.

**Install the glass.** Once everything is finished, install the glass using small strips of cherry (⅛" and ¼" thick). A few dabs of clear silicone and a couple small pins do the trick.

**TRAY JOINERY**

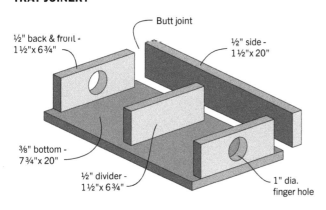

Butt joint

½" back & front -
1 ½"x 6 ¾"

½" side -
1 ½"x 20"

⅜" bottom -
7 ¾"x 20"

½" divider -
1 ½"x 6 ¾"

1" dia.
finger hole

**SMALL DRAWER JOINERY**

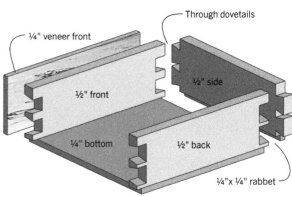

Through dovetails

¼" veneer front

½" side

½" front

¼" bottom

½" back

¼"x ¼" rabbet

## CUT LIST & MATERIALS

| | NO. | ITEM | DIMENSIONS (INCHES) | | | MATERIAL | COMMENTS |
|---|---|---|---|---|---|---|---|
| | | | T | W | L | | |
| ☐ | 2 | Carcase sides | ¾ | 12 ¼ | 33 | Cherry | ⅜"-deep x 1"-wide rabbet at back. |
| ☐ | 2 | Carcase top rails | ¾ | 3 | 24 | Cherry | Dovetailed into sides. |
| ☐ | 1 | Bottom | ¾ | 11 ¼ | 24 | Cherry | Dovetailed into sides. |
| ☐ | 1 | Top cap | 1 | 17 | 32 | Cherry | ½"-deep x 3"-wide bevel. |
| ☐ | | Shiplapped back | ½ | 23 ¼ | 33 | Ambrosia maple | ¼" x ¼" shiplaps. |
| ☐ | 2 | French cleats | ½ | 5 | 24 | Poplar | |
| ☐ | 1 | Major horizontal divider | ¾ | 10 ½ | 23 | Cherry | In ¼"-deep x ½"-wide dados. |
| ☐ | 1 | Top horizontal divider | ½ | 10 ½ | 23 | Cherry | In ¼"-deep x ½"-wide dados. |
| ☐ | 3 | Thin horizontal dividers | ½ | 9 ¼ | 23 | Cherry | In ¼"-deep x ½"-wide dados. |
| ☐ | 5 | Vertical dividers | ½ | 10 | 6 ½ | Cherry | In ⅛"-deep x ½"-wide dados. |
| ☐ | 2 | Small vertical dividers | ½ | 9 ¼ | 2 ¾ | Cherry | In ⅛"-deep x ½"-wide dados. |
| ☐ | 2 | Door large stiles | ¾ | 2 ¾ | 33 | Cherry | |
| ☐ | 2 | Door small stiles | ¾ | 1 ¼ | 33 | Cherry | |
| ☐ | 2 | Door top rails | ¾ | 2 ¾ | 10 | Cherry | 1" TBE† |
| ☐ | 2 | Door intermediate rails | ¾ | 2 ¼ | 10 | Cherry | 1" TBE† |
| ☐ | 2 | Door lower rails | ¾ | 3 ¾ | 10 | Cherry | 1" TBE† |
| ☐ | 2 | Door panels | ½ | 8 ½ | 16 ¾ | Spalted maple | In ¼"-wide x ⅜"-deep groove. |
| ☐ | 2 | Vertical muntins | ¼ | ½ | 8 | Cherry | |
| ☐ | 4 | Horizontal muntins | ¼ | ½ | 3 ¾ | Cherry | |
| ☐ | 2 | Backing strips | ¼ | ½ | 8 ½ | Cherry | In ¼"-wide x ½"-deep rabbet, glued to vertical muntin. |
| ☐ | 4 | Small backing strips | ¼ | ½ | 4 ⅛ | Cherry | Glued to horizontal muntin. |

## MEDIUM AND LARGE DRAWER JOINERY

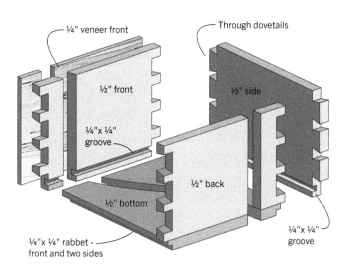

¼" veneer front

Through dovetails

½" front

½" side

¼"x ¼" groove

½" back

½" bottom

¼"x ¼" rabbet - front and two sides

¼"x ¼" groove

drawers on the left edge of the cabinet are a tad wider than the reveals on the right side. And in a couple of the dovetails at the rear of the drawers, there are a couple small gaps. It's not perfect.

But before I got too down on myself, I remembered one more quote from Ruskin that relates to handwork and the pursuit of perfection. This one deserves as much ink as the first.

"No good work whatever can be perfect," he writes, "and the demand for perfection is always a sign of a misunderstanding of the ends of art." ▪

## CUT LIST & MATERIALS CONTINUED

| | NO. | ITEM | T | W | L | MATERIAL | COMMENTS |
|---|---|---|---|---|---|---|---|
| ☐ | 8 | Window panes | | | | Glass | Cut to fit openings. |
| ☐ | 1 | Window backing strips | ⅛ | ¼ | 62 | Cherry | Cut to trap panes. |
| ☐ | 4 | Small drawer fronts | ¾* | 2½ | 11 | Poplar/Spalted maple | ¼"-deep x ½" rabbet on bottom edge. |
| ☐ | 8 | Small drawer sides | ½ | 2½ | 9 | Poplar | ¼"-deep x ¼" rabbet on bottom edge. |
| ☐ | 4 | Small drawer backs | ½ | 2¼ | 11 | Poplar | |
| ☐ | 4 | Small drawer bottoms | ¼ | 10½ | 9 | Plywood | Screwed to drawer box. |
| ☐ | 1 | Medium drawer front | ¾* | 5 | 22½ | Poplar/Spalted maple | ¼"-deep x ¼"-wide groove for bottom. |
| ☐ | 2 | Medium drawer sides | ½ | 5 | 9 | Poplar | ¼"-deep x ¼"-wide groove for bottom. |
| ☐ | 1 | Medium drawer back | ½ | 4½ | 22½ | Poplar | |
| ☐ | 1 | Medium drawer bottom | ½ | 8¾ | 22 | Plywood | ¼"-deep x ¼" rabbet on bottom edge. |
| ☐ | 1 | Large drawer front | ¾* | 6¾ | 22½ | Poplar/Spalted maple | ¼"-deep x ¼"-wide groove for bottom. |
| ☐ | 2 | Large drawer sides | ½ | 6¾ | 9 | Poplar | ¼"-deep x ¼"-wide groove for bottom. |
| ☐ | 1 | Large drawer back | ½ | 6½ | 22½ | Poplar | |
| ☐ | 1 | Large drawer bottom | ½ | 8¾ | 22 | Plywood | ¼"-deep x ¼" rabbet on bottom edge. |
| ☐ | 6 | Traditional ring pulls | | 28 mm | | Iron | |
| ☐ | 2 | Traditional ring pulls | | 40 mm | | Iron | |
| ☐ | 2 | Traditional ring pulls | | 50 mm | | Iron | |
| ☐ | 6 | Unequal strap hinges | | | | | 9½" (decorative leaf width) x 5" (mounting leaf width). |
| ☐ | 4 | Magnetic catches | | | | | |

* Finished dimension, laminated from ½" poplar front and ¼" spalted maple veneer. † TBE = tenon, both ends. Build drawer trays and dividers as desired.

# CONTRIBUTORS

Abraham, Jameel: "Traveling Tool Chest" (Lid, p. 42)

Blackburn, Graham: "Portable Chisel Rack" (Illus., p. 120)

Ciarcia, Joe: "Tommy Mac's Toolbox" (Photog., p. 100)

Cleveland, Eli: "Tommy Mac's Toolbox" (Model, p. 100)

Day, Austin: "Dovetailed, Curly Maple Tool Chest" (Photog., p. 74)

Dillinger, Zachary: "Machinist's Tool Chest" (Author/Photog., p. 66)

Fidgen, Tom: "One for the Road" (Author, p. 51)

Fitzpatrick, Megan: "Tool Tote" (Author, p. 6)

Hennessey, Chris: "Dovetailed, Curly Maple Tool Chest" (Photog., p. 74)

Huey, Glen D.: "Hardware Hideaway" (Author, p. 16)
"Not-So-Ordinary Router Cabinet" (Author/Photog., p. 168)

Lang, Robert W.: "Cabinet Maker's Tool Chest" (Author, p. 157)
"Not-So-Ordinary Router Cabinet" (Illus., p. 168)
"Tommy Mac's Toolbox" (Illus., p. 100)
"Tool Rack" (Illus., p. 125)

Lyell, David: "A Traveler's Tool Case" (Author, p. 23)

Macdonald, Thomas J.: "Tommy Mac's Toolbox" (Author, p. 100)

Nayar, Narayan: "12 Rules for Tool Chests" (Lead Photog., p. 91)

Parrish, Al: "Arts & Crafts Tool Cabinet" (Photog., p. 178)
"Not-So-Ordinary Router Cabinet" (Lead Photog., p. 168)
"Tool Rack" (Lead Photog., p. 125)
"Traveling Tool Chest" (Lead Photog., p. 42)

Pessell, Dan: "Traveling Tool Chest" (Illus., p. 42)

Rainford, Bill: "Authentic Sloyd Tool Cabinet" (Author, p. 27)

Schwarz, Christopher: "12 Rules for Tool Chests" (Author/Photog./Illus., p. 91)
"Arts & Crafts Tool Cabinet" (Author, p. 178)
"Dutch Tool Chest" (Author/Photog., p. 108)
"Handplane Cabinet" (Author/Photog., p. 146)
"Portable Chisel Rack" (Author, p. 120)
"Roy Underhill's Nail Cabinet" (Author, p. 137)
"Tool Rack" (Author/Photog., p. 125)
"Traveling Tool Chest" (Author/Photog., p. 42)

Siemsen, Mike: "Saw & Plane Till" (Author/Photog., p. 129)

Stack, Jim: "10-Drawer Tool Chest" (Author, p. 84)

Stanton, Chad: "Stacking Tool Caddy" (Author, p. 9)

Weber, Don: "Traveling Toolbox" (Author, p. 58)

Wittmer, Logan: "Dovetailed, Curly Maple Tool Chest" (Author, p. 74)

Zoellner, Andrew: "A Traveler's Tool Case" (Author, p. 23)

# MANUFACTURERS

Visit your local woodworking store or look online for these brands mentioned in the book.

Ball & Ball (reproduction hardware) ballandball.com

Beadalon (wire bending jig) www.beadalon.com

Black Bear Forge (hardware) www.blackbearforge.com

Fine Box Hardware (hinges) www.fineboxhardware.com

Freud (box joint cutter set) www.freudtools.com

Horton Brasses, Inc. (furniture nails, reproduction hardware) horton-brasses.com

Micro-Mark (wire bending jig) www.micromark.com

Peter Ross Blacksmithing (hinges, hardware) peterrossblacksmith.com

Stanley Tools (plane) www.stanleytools.com

Tremont Nail Co. (brads) tremontnail.com

Whitechapel Ltd. (hardware) whitechapel-ltd.com

# INDEX

3D printer 41

arc 8, 85, 86, 87, 172

backsaw holders 56
blowout prevention 25
box joints. *See* finger joints
braces 68
breadboard ends 32, 96, 113

chamfer 6, 7, 20, 30, 61, 82, 122, 124, 127, 184
chest lifts 48
compass 8, 101, 102, 172, 183
Craftsman 85

divider 13, 14, 15, 141
door, build a better 174
dovetails 25, 43, 44, 49, 52, 55, 72, 77, 94, 101–106, 109, 110, 130–133, 140, 148–152, 158, 161, 162, 164, 169, 170, 182–184, 186, 187
dowel joinery 67
drawer 32–35, 69–71, 89, 106, 114, 132–133, 143–144, 163–164, 173, 175, 180, 181, 186–189
drawer pulls 73, 85, 90, 105, 107, 164, 166, 175

egg-crate joint 18, 139

fall-front 109–113
finger joints 16, 29, 32, 139, 140, 163, 164
finishing 15, 22, 31, 32, 41, 50, 73, 83, 99, 107, 113, 124, 128, 136, 144, 156, 167
French cleat 144, 156, 167, 183

gang-cut 43, 110, 132, 139

handles 6–8, 13–15, 34, 48, 56, 73
hide glue 32, 33, 79, 140, 162
hinges 22, 34, 36, 49, 54, 60, 82, 109, 112, 142, 155, 156, 167, 176, 185

jig 19, 30, 170, 183

lock 34, 36, 37, 49, 96, 111, 113, 167, 173
muntins 184, 185, 188

North Bennet Street School 27, 100, 192

ogee 48, 73, 126, 173

painter's tape 11, 25, 76
planes, positioning 151
planes, waxing 153
plugs 85, 87, 90, 172, 173

rabbeted dovetails 49
rabbets 11, 67, 102–103, 106, 164, 169–171, 182
rack 48, 81, 97, 114, 120, 124, 166, 167, 180
raised-panel door 96
ramp block 104
rot strips 44
rubbed joint 60
rules for tool chests 91
runners 29, 46, 47, 69, 94, 98

sacrificial fence 17, 29, 32, 173
Shaker 126, 128
shiplap 22, 48, 184
shooting board 52, 57
skirt 46, 49, 50, 95
sliding lid 52
Sloyd 3, 27–41
spring joints 101
spring latch, depressor 14
stop block 6, 10, 34, 164
strap hinges 109, 112, 185, 189

through-mortises 7
through-tenons 6
tills 48, 54–56, 97, 115, 129, 181
Tolpin, Jim 179, 192
tool holders, making 37–40
tote 6, 7, 9, 75, 92
trammel 7, 8, 85

Underhill, Roy 51, 109, 137

Text and photographs © 2022

Publisher: Paul McGahren
Editorial Director: Kerri Grzybicki
Design & Layout: Clare Finney

Cedar Lane Press
PO Box 5424
Lancaster, PA 17606-5424

Paperback ISBN: 978-1-950934-86-7
ePub ISBN: 978-1-950934-87-4

Library of Congress Control Number: 2022934384

Printed in the United States of America
10 9 8 7 6 5 4 3 2 1

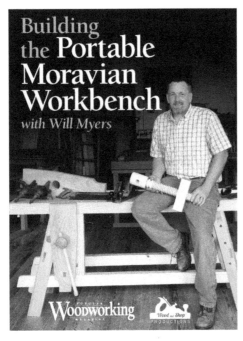
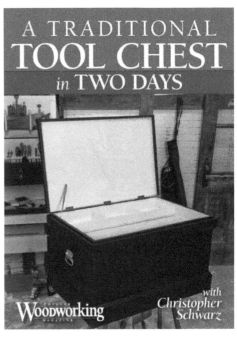

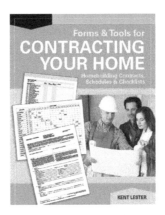
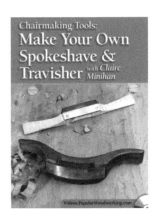

CPSIA information can be obtained
at www.ICGtesting.com
Printed in the USA
JSHW061403241022
31970JS00001B/1